T0164016

THE NATURAL HISTORY OF
INSECTS

THE NATURAL HISTORY OF
INSECTS

A guide to the world of arthropods, covering many insect orders, including beetles, flies, stick insects, dragonflies, ants and wasps, as well as microscopic creatures

Features 140 photographs and more than 30 specially commissioned illustrations of the habits, life cycles and habitats of many insect species, including spiders

MARTIN WALTERS

southwater

This edition is published by Southwater,
an imprint of Anness Publishing Ltd,
Blaby Road, Wigston,
Leicestershire LE18 4SE;
info@anness.com

www.southwaterbooks.com www.annesspublishing.com

If you like the images in this book and would like to investigate using them for publishing, promotions or
advertising, please visit our website www.practicalpictures.com for
more information.

Publisher: Joanna Lorenz
Editorial Director: Helen Sudell
Editors: Simona Hill, Anne Hildyard
Book and cover design: Nigel Partridge
Illustrators: Andrey Atuchin, Penny Brown,
Peter Bull, Stuart Jackson-Carter,
Felicity Cole, Joanne Glover, Paul Jones,
Jonathan Latimer, Carol Mullin,
Fiona Osbaldstone, Denys Ovenden
Production Controller: TBC

© Anness Publishing Ltd 2013

All rights reserved. No part of this publication may be reproduced, stored in a retrieval system, or transmitted in
any way or by any means, electronic, mechanical, photocopying, recording or otherwise, without the prior written
permission of the copyright holder.

ACKNOWLEDGEMENTS
The author would like to thank the following people for their help with researching information: Yvonne Barnett,
Sarah Hart, Virginie Mellot, Jane Parker, Steve Parker, Leanne Scott.

PUBLISHER'S NOTE
Although the advice and information in this book are believed to be accurate and true at the time of going to
press, neither the authors nor the publisher can accept any legal responsibility or liability for any errors or
omissions that may have been made.

CONTENTS

INTRODUCTION

Insects are all around us – in our immediate surroundings, in our homes and gardens, even sometimes on our own bodies. They are the most successful group of living creatures on Earth, and have colonized almost every habitat known, with the exception of the seas, where very few are found. From cold mountain terrain to damp riverbanks and at every altitude and temperature zone, every type of landscape is host to a myriad insect species, each playing a vital role in the ecological balance. Each species has adapted to survive in its habitat as well as alongside other species of animal and plant, and it is partly these adaptations that make insects such a fascinating group of creatures to study.

It is easy to dismiss insects as unpleasant creepy-crawlies, and it is true that some make an irritating buzzing, or have a feeding habit or life cycle that causes damage to crops and even furniture, and the relatively few that bite us or sting are a nuisance, some even spreading dangerous diseases. But insects in all their variety are collectively more beneficial than harmful to human society. In fact, there are plenty of insects that play a vital role in our food chain, as well as others that add to the aesthetic appeal of the great outdoors. For these reasons, it is worth paying closer attention to these fascinating creatures that share our world.

Above: This beetle has a formidable set of antlers that act as its primary defence against other insects. It uses them to jostle with other beetles.

Most insects are relatively small, and while a louse or flea may look dissimilar to a butterfly, insects do share certain characteristics. The typical adult insect has three pairs of legs and normally two pairs of wings, with a body normally divided into three distinct sections: head, thorax and abdomen. The insect head has mouthparts (which may be specialized for chewing, biting or sucking), eyes (which may be simple or compound) and antennae. The insect uses its antennae to sense vibrations or chemicals in the environment.

Identification

Everyone is familiar with flies, bees, dragonflies, beetles, butterflies, grasshoppers and bugs, as well as a whole host of other common creatures, and many are easy to identify. Sit a while in a small area of land such as a flower meadow, a railway embankment, or

Left: This hoverfly shows the typical features of an insect's body: three sets of legs, two sets of wings, and a body divided into three parts, made up of the head, upper body or thorax and lower body or abdomen.

near a garden pond and before long the presence of insects will become apparent. Being able to identify individual insect species takes time however, and in the case of large orders with many species this is really the province of the expert entomologist. In addition, many species will not stay around long enough for you to get your identification guidebook turned to the correct page before they have moved on. Having a camera to be able to take a photograph helps the process of identification, as does a notepad in which to make any obvious notes of body shape, markings, approximate size and colouring. Knowing what species to expect in a given area helps too. That way you will know when you have seen something truly remarkable in the area that you are visiting. Some insects, for example, are attracted to specific plants for the nectar and pollen that they produce.

With one million known insect species named, and many more awaiting identification, it would be impossible to do justice to such amazing diversity in a single volume. Instead this book aims to present a selection of the most common, as well as unusual species from around the globe. There will be plenty of insects presented here that you may recognize without too much difficulty. Other insects are fascinating because of their unusual behaviour or appearance, some for example mimicking other insects in order to avoid detection by predators. Some, such as many butterflies and moths, are beautiful, with their delicate, attractively coloured scales, while others, such as some of the larger beetles, are remarkably bulky. Included too are some other common members of the phylum Arthropoda, such as spiders, mites, ticks, millipedes and centipedes

Above: Dragonflies' wings are held open when at rest.

Below: Butterflies can reach up to 30cm (12in) across in some tropical countries and appear in a limitless range of colours. They have the most dramatic life cycle of all the insects.

UNDERSTANDING INSECTS

Insects form the most diverse group of animals on Earth. They are extremely successful and, despite their small size, they affect many aspects of our lives. Insects may live on land or in water, although only a small number are known to inhabit the oceans. Insects in all their varied forms belong, along with crustaceans (crabs, lobsters, shrimps, woodlice etc), arachnids (spiders, scorpions etc) and myriapods (millipedes and centipedes), to a group known as arthropods. This group is the largest phylum of the animal kingdom. The word comes from the Greek and means 'jointed-limbed', a feature common to all members of this phylum.

This chapter aims to give an overview of insects, their evolution and development, and the way scientists have classified them into different orders. Insects have a common anatomical make-up and this is described and illustrated, with particular adaptations, such as antennae, highlighted. The life stages of insects are featured and shown too, including the metamorphosis from egg to larva, pupa and adult, where appropriate. There is discussion on how insects organize themselves, living in colonies and working for the collective group, or living solitary lives. Each order has adapted different mechanisms for self-defence, as well as methods of camouflage against predation, and in order to fool its prey, and these are all looked at in detail.The power of flight is another key feature of most insects and has enabled them to live active and mobile lives.

Left: A bumblebee feeds on nectar from a thistle. In return for this sugary meal it carries pollen to another thistle flower.

WHAT ARE INSECTS?

There are five features that are common to all insects, and which may be the key to the success of these amazing animals. These features are a tough outer skeleton, small size, adaptability, the power of flight (in some species) and metamorphosis (changing body shape).

Insects are fascinating creatures and account for more than three-quarters of all known animals. For example there are about 90,000 species of insect in North America, and a similar number in Europe. Some of the most common insects are flies, wasps, beetles, ants, crickets and grasshoppers. They are often persecuted as pests or dismissed as ordinary 'creepy-crawlies'. However, many people love them and there is a great deal left to be learned about them. Many insects exist in enormous numbers, for example ants, gnats and termites. Being small, they are able to colonize areas quickly, and also reproduce at a fast rate.

Insects also play an important role in the economy of nature. They pollinate plants, serve as food for other animals and dispose of dead organisms, as well as doing many other ecologically essential tasks, such as the recycling of organic matter. On the downside, many insects, such as mosquitoes and locusts, transmit diseases and damage crops, but the good services that most insects offer greatly outweigh the harm caused by the few destructive ones.

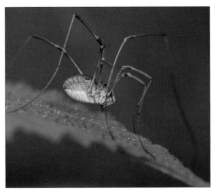

Insects may have gregarious or solitary social lifestyles and may be conspicuous, mimics of other objects, such as leaves or other forms of natural life, or they live concealed and camouflaged. They may also be active by day or night. Due to their life cycle, insects are able to survive under a wide range of conditions, such as extreme heat or cold, and have adapted to survive in all habitats except the ocean. The following five features are characteristic of insects.

The exoskeleton

Insects, like other arthropods, possess a tough outer skeleton made of a special protein called chitin. This layer

Left: The harvestman is an arachnid, rather than an insect. Unlike insects it has four pairs of legs. Spiders and scorpions are also arachnids, a subphylum of arthropods.

protects the body and enables them to survive in extreme environments. The exoskeleton also restricts water loss and because of this it has freed insects from the necessity to live in damp places and allowed them to move into a wide range of habitats on land.

Size

Compared with most other animals, most insects are fairly small, with many having body lengths of just 1–10mm (0.04–0.39in) (although some, such as stick insects, can reach 30cm (12in) in length. Wingspans range between 0.5mm (0.02in) and 30cm (12in). Insects that are unusually long or have a greater wingspan than most still have quite slender bodies. The largest insects are usually found in tropical areas.

The small size of insects can be attributed mainly to their breathing mechanism. Insects use a different breathing system from that of vertebrates and most other groups of invertebrate animals. Insect respiration is accomplished without lungs but instead via a system of internal tubes and sacs through which gases either diffuse or are actively pumped, delivering oxygen to all the parts of the body. Since the circulatory system of an insect is not used to carry oxygen, it is small and simplified. It consists of little more than a single, perforated dorsal tube, which circulates the liquid inside the body through muscular pumping movements.

Small size is a great advantage to insects when it comes to finding places to live. It enables them to colonize tiny places that larger creatures are totally unable to access. Tough, but also light, many insects fly or drift long distances.

Below: Insects have six legs, a body divided into three parts, and often have wings and the ability to fly. This is a hoverfly.

Below: Unlike insects, myriapods have many pairs of legs. They include centipedes and millipedes.

Above: Some insects spend the time between larval and adult stages as a pupa.

Adaptability

There are very few places on Earth that have not been inhabited by insects. They survive in a range of habitats, from mountain-tops and hot deserts to lakes and rivers. Their adaptability on land seems almost unlimited. Some of the most important adaptations in insects are related to their feeding habits. For example, their jaws can deal with a wide range of foods, both solid and liquid. In fact, there are few organic materials that are immune to insect attack. Most plants play host to one or more species.

Below: Woodlice are crustaceans, not insects, and are classified together with crabs and lobsters.

Insects can feed off plants that are poisonous to humans and other animals. Some feed off animals, eating smaller creatures and sucking the blood of larger ones, while others survive by living off unlikely foods such as dung, furniture or clothes.

Flight

Insects are the only group of invertebrates to have developed flight. Being able to fly allows insects to escape from predators more effectively, find mates more easily and move long distances to find their feeding grounds.

Metamorphosis

As they mature, most insects change their body shape, a process known as metamorphosis. The most abundant and successful insects are those which undergo complete metamorphosis. This

Above: Damselflies are among the many winged insects.

is when the larvae are totally different in appearance from the adults. The reason for this success is because while the insects are at differing stages of development, they survive on different kinds of food. For example, a caterpillar will live on a diet of leaves, but as an adult butterfly it sips nectar.

These five factors of toughness, small size, adaptability, flight and metamorphosis, along with others, such as the ability to quickly reproduce, all contribute to the abundance and success of the members of this amazing group.

Below: Moths use their powerful wings to fly from flower to flower collecting nectar and spreading pollen.

EVOLUTION OF INSECTS

Evolution has produced an astonishing variety of insects. Most of the major orders of insects alive today were already distinguishable 250 million years ago. They first appeared in the fossil record 400 million years ago and have continued to evolve and adapt ever since.

The oldest known insect fossil is *Rhyniognatha hirsti*, believed to be about 400 million years old. This fossil was found in red sandstone in Scotland in rocks dated at between 396 and 407 million years old. Its existence suggests that insects probably evolved in the Silurian Period (412–438 million years ago). *R. hirsti* possessed insect-like mandibles rather like those of winged insects today, suggesting that wings may have already evolved by this time.

By the Carboniferous Period (290–355 million years ago), different kinds of insects had evolved. The most ancient winged insects probably included primitive cockroaches, whose fossils date back to the late Devonian Period (370 million years ago). Their early appearance shows the significance of a scavenging lifestyle in terms of adaptability. By about 300 million years ago these insects were diverse. The members of this order varied in size and morphology, most notably in mouthparts, wing articulation and the pattern of veins in the wings.

An early origin of plant feeding is indicated by the beak-like, piercing mouthparts of some Carboniferous insects. It was in the Permian Period (250–290 million years ago) that conifers became abundant in a flora that was previously dominated by

Above: Fossils show that many insect groups that thrive today, such as this cricket, lived millions of years ago.

ferns. A dramatic increase in insect diversity is seen in this period, with 30 orders known to exist by that time. Newly available plants may have had something to do with the evolution of the plant-sucking true bugs (Hemiptera). Other insects in the Permian included those that fed on pollen, another resource that had previously been unavailable.

Giant insects

Some Carboniferous and Permian insects were large, and included giant dragonflies and mayflies. Wingspans of up to 71cm (28in) have been recorded on fossils of these gigantic insects. A possible explanation for this large size is that there may have been higher

levels of oxygen in the atmosphere at that time and that this made for more efficient diffusion in the insects' breathing tubes. The size of modern insects is restricted by the difficulties of getting enough oxygen to their muscles. If other gases were unchanged, the extra atmospheric oxygen would have made the air denser than it is today, making flight for larger creatures easier.

Some early medium to large insects disappeared at the end of the Permian, while others including the mayflies (Ephemeroptera), dragonflies and damselflies (Odonata), stoneflies (Plecoptera), wingless insects (Grylloblattodea), crickets and grass-hoppers (Orthoptera), and cockroaches and mantids (Dictyoptera) survived. The phase between the Permian and Triassic Periods was one of major extinction that dramatically reduced diversity within the insect orders.

Insects of the dinosaur era

The Triassic (205–250 million years ago) is best known for the appearance of dinosaurs and mammals. By the beginning of the period, the major orders of modern insects, apart from the sawflies, wasps, bees, ants, and moths and butterflies, were established. The order Hymenoptera was only weakly represented in this period by sawflies and wood wasps. The appearance of the oldest still-living families occurred in this period, including modern dragonflies and damselflies, true bugs and true flies.

In the Jurassic Period (135–205 million years ago), bees, wasps and ants and many forms of true flies appeared. In the Cretaceous Period (65–135 million years ago), many insects and other arthropods were

Left: Many modern-day insects can be traced back to the era of the dinosaurs.

preserved in exuded tree resin that occasionally trapped insects and then turned into a clear fossilized substance known as amber. In comparison to stone fossils, which may have consisted of little more than a crumpled body or wing, this process preserved whole insects.

The rapid increase and diversification of insects in the Cretaceous Period coincides with the diversification of flowering plant species (angiosperms).

However, the evolution of the major mouthpart types seen in insects today occurred before the appearance of flowering plants.

Modern insects

Some fossils from the Cretaceous Period are so similar to modern insects that they have been able to be classified in existing genera. Much of our knowledge of more modern

insects, from the Tertiary Period (65–1.8 million years ago), comes from amber fossils.

All northern temperate, subarctic and arctic zone fossil insects, many of which are beetles, dating from the last million years, appear to be almost identical to existing species. Climatic variations in the last 1.8 million years have seemingly caused many changes in the ranges of existing species.

Insect evolution

This diagram shows the possible relationships of the major insect orders and the approximate geological times during which they are thought to have arisen. Note, however, that insect classification is complex and the relationships of the groups and their ages are constantly being modified in the light of new research.

Key

1 Collembola (Springtails)
2 Diplura (Diplurans)
3 Protura (Proturans)
4 Archaeognatha (Bristletails) and
    Thysanura (Silverfish)
5 Ephemeroptera (Mayflies)
6 Odonata (Dragonflies and
    Damselflies)
7 Grylloblattodea (Rock Crawlers)
8 Plecoptera (Stoneflies)
9 Zoraptera (Zorapterans)
10 Embioptera (Web Spinners)
11 Dermaptera (Earwigs)
12 Isoptera (Termites)
13 Blattodea (Cockroaches)
14 Mantodea (Mantids)
15 Phasmatodea (Stick and
    Leaf Insects)
16 Orthoptera (Crickets and
    Grasshoppers)
17 Psocoptera (Booklice and Bark-lice)
18 Phthiraptera (Parasitic Lice)
19 Thysanoptera (Thrips)
20 Hemiptera (True Bugs)
21 Neuroptera (Lacewings),
    Megaloptera (Alder-flies and
    Dobsonflies), Raphidioptera
    (Snake Flies)
22 Mecoptera (Scorpion Flies)
23 Trichoptera (Caddis Flies)
24 Lepidoptera (Butterflies and
    Moths)
25 Siphonaptera (Fleas)
26 Diptera (Flies)
27 Strepsiptera (Strepsipterans)
28 Hymenoptera (Bees, Wasps,
    Ants and Sawflies)
29 Coleoptera (Beetles)

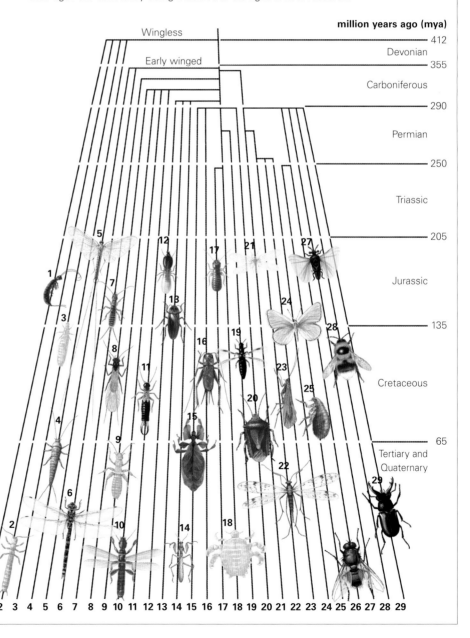

Wingless
Early winged

million years ago (mya)
412
Devonian
355
Carboniferous
290
Permian
250
Triassic
205
Jurassic
135
Cretaceous
65
Tertiary and
Quaternary

1 2 3 4 5 6 7 8 9 10 11 12 13 14 15 16 17 18 19 20 21 22 23 24 25 26 27 28 29

CLASSIFICATION OF INSECTS

The creatures that make up the animal kingdom are arranged into phyla according to their characteristics. Arthropoda is the largest phylum. It can be divided into four classes: Insecta, Crustacea (crabs and relatives), Arachnida (spiders and relatives), and Myriapoda (centipedes and millipedes).

The class Insecta contains almost one million species, split into two subclasses: wingless insects and winged insects. These two groups are further subdivided into different orders.

The orders that make up the class Insecta are primarily the focus of our interest in this book and make up the majority of entries in the regional directory. However, the most common creatures from the other three classes of Arthropoda are also included, such as the wingless near-insects. These creatures share some features with true insects, such as number of legs, and are often thought of as being insects, such as spiders and millipedes.

THE CLASS INSECTA

Bristletails (Order Archaeognatha)
Small, wingless insects with flexible bodies, and thread-like bristles at the tail.

Silverfish (Order Thysanura)
Similar to bristletails but often with a shiny, silvery sheen and flattened, tapering body.

Mayflies (Order Ephemeroptera)
Primitive insects with two pairs of wings, a long body with a number of 'tails' and a brief adult lifespan.

Dragonflies and Damselflies (Order Odonata)
Primitive slim-bodied adults with two pairs of wings, biting mouthparts and large compound eyes for hunting aerial prey.

Gladiators (Order Mantophasmatodea)
Only discovered in 2002, this small group of wingless insects live in southern and eastern Africa.

Cockroaches (Order Blattodea)
Adults (and most nymph stages) have a flattened body with an enlarged pronotum body, compound eyes and strong biting jaws.

Termites (Order Isoptera)
The body consists of a soft cuticle with a harder area on the head. Highly social. Reproductively active adults have wings while workers and soldiers do not.

Mantids (Order Mantodea)
Characteristic triangular shaped, downward-facing head with large eyes. Predatory habits aided by modified forelegs and cryptic coloration.

Rock Crawlers (Order Grylloblattodea)
Another small group of wingless insects, related to stick insects. They live in high mountains in western North America and eastern Asia.

Web Spinners (Order Embioptera)
Brown, soft-bodied insects with biting jaws on a broad head; males have two pairs of wings; females are wingless.

Stick and Leaf Insects (Order Phasmatodea)
Long, slender or flattened insects with biting mouthparts. May or may not have wings. Usually shaped in the form of vegetation (leaf or twigs).

Earwigs (Order Dermaptera)
Long antennae, a slender, flattened body (some winged) and enlarged pincer-shaped appendages (cerci) on the rear end (though absent in some).

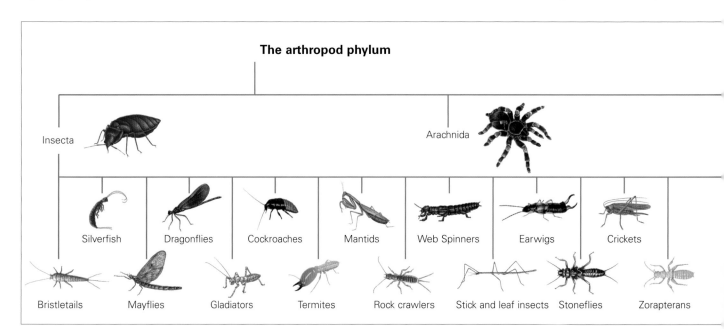

The arthropod phylum

Insecta — Arachnida

Silverfish — Dragonflies — Cockroaches — Mantids — Web Spinners — Earwigs — Crickets

Bristletails — Mayflies — Gladiators — Termites — Rock crawlers — Stick and leaf insects — Stoneflies — Zorapterans

Stoneflies (Order Plecoptera)
Primitive insects with two pairs of wings, a cylindrical body and segmented, thread-like tails.

Crickets and Grasshoppers (Order Orthoptera)
Stout, rigid-bodied insects with large modified hind legs.

Zorapterans (Order Zoraptera)
Tiny insects with soft bodies, long antennae, biting mouthparts, an enlarged prothorax and, in some species, wings.

Booklice (Order Psocoptera)
Small, soft-bodied insects which hold their wings in a tent shape at rest (although some are wingless). Usually 1–2mm (0.04–0.08in) long.

Thrips (Order Thysanoptera)
Tiny insects (most less than 2mm (0.08in) long) with long, thin, soft bodies, piercing and sucking mouthparts, sensitive antennae, and some species also bearing two pairs of hair-fringed wings.

Parasitic Lice (Order Phthiraptera)
Flattened, wingless, often with strong claws, one pair of spiracles (the opening through which oxygen enters the body) on the side surface, short antennae and a range of mouthparts.

Bugs (Order Hemiptera)
Insects with specialized piercing and sucking mouthparts (rostrum and stylets); body shape and size vary.

Snake Flies (Order Raphidioptera)
Long-necked (enlarged prothorax) predatory insects with four wings and bristle-like antennae.

Alder-flies (Order Megaloptera)
Biting mouthparts and four wings which join together.

Lacewings (Order Neuroptera)
A diverse order of insects with sucking mouthparts, long antennae, four clearly veined wings, large compound eyes and an often 'hairy' appearance.

Beetles (Order Coleoptera)
The dorsal area of body has adapted forewings creating hard wing cases (elytra) for the protection of underlying wings. Biting mouthparts.

Strepsipterans (Order Strepsiptera)
Minute insects with biting mouthparts and adult males (when present, as some species are parthenogenetic) with broad membranous hindwings.

Fleas (Order Siphonaptera)
Wingless, with laterally flattened bodies, bloodsucking mouthparts and powerful hind legs.

Scorpion Flies (Order Mecoptera)
Front of head projects down into a pointed beak with biting parts at the end; two pairs of wings; abdomen tip in males often curved upward creating the appearance of a scorpion sting.

Flies (Order Diptera)
Most species usually have two membranous wings for flight and a second reduced pair of 'halteres' for balance. Mouthparts adapted for sucking or piercing; varied appearance with many examples of mimicry.

Caddis Flies (Order Trichoptera)
These insects have two pairs of membranous wings (less veined than lacewings, though superficially similar to some species).

Butterflies (Order Lepidoptera)
Adult mouthparts are usually reduced to a proboscis which coils away neatly when not in use. The wings are covered in a wide variety of distinct overlapping, often very colourful, scales.

Bees, Wasps, Ants and Sawflies (Order Hymenoptera)
These species usually have two pairs of membranous wings (with the front pair being larger) joined by hooks; chewing mouthparts. Ants are mainly wingless, except for reproductives.

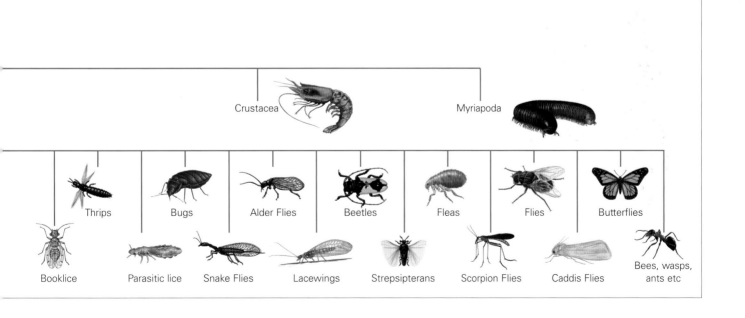

Crustacea   Myriapoda

Thrips   Bugs   Alder Flies   Beetles   Fleas   Flies   Butterflies

Booklice   Parasitic lice   Snake Flies   Lacewings   Strepsipterans   Scorpion Flies   Caddis Flies   Bees, wasps, ants etc

INSECT ANATOMY

The body of an adult insect consists of three main parts – the head, thorax (upper body) and abdomen (lower body). Even though insect species can look vastly different to each other in scale and make up, they all have a common body configuration.

An insect's body is segmented with usually 20 similar rings or segments. There are six segments in the head, three in the thorax and eleven in the abdomen. Some may be fused together. The main part of the body wall is the cuticle, a major component of which is chitin. Chitin is a protein that forms up to 60 per cent of the cuticle's dry weight. A process called tanning brings about hardening of the cuticle. Tough plates called sclerites are formed in most segments as a result. The cuticle remains soft and flexible between the segments, forming joints that enable the body to move.

The head
An insect's head is a tough capsule. It supports a pair of sensory antennae, a pair of compound (complex) eyes, one to three simple eyes and three sets of variously modified appendages that form the mouthparts, usually specialized for sucking or biting.

The antennae are mainly concerned with the senses of smell and touch. They are composed of numerous separate segments. Most insects have compound and simple eyes, but in some species, one set of these may be missing. Compound eyes are larger and more conspicuous than simple eyes, the latter merely distinguishing light from dark.

The thorax
An insect's thorax is the middle section of the body. The three segments that make up the thorax are named, from front to back, the prothorax, mesothorax and metathorax. A pair of legs is present on each segment while the mesothorax and metathorax carry the wings. The forewings are

Below: A cockroach is a typical insect. Some species have wings, although this species lacks them. As with all insects, the body is divided into three parts: the head, the thorax and the abdomen. These, in turn, are subdivided into smaller sections.

normally larger than the hindwings and are found on the mesothorax, which in consequence is normally larger than the metathorax. Almost all adult insects have six legs. The basic structure of the leg comprises the coxa (which articulates with the thorax), the trochanter (small and movable on the coxa but firmly fixed to the femur), the femur (the largest segment), the tibia (which often carries a number of spines), and the tarsus.

The wings
Functional insect wings are membranous, transparent projections that are supported and strengthened by a network of veins. The same basic wing pattern of veins is consistent within families and orders and, as such, is useful in insect classification and identification. The textures of both pairs of wings are generally quite similar; however, in some insects, such as beetles and bugs, they are sometimes different, with the forewings being tougher in order to protect the softer hindwings.

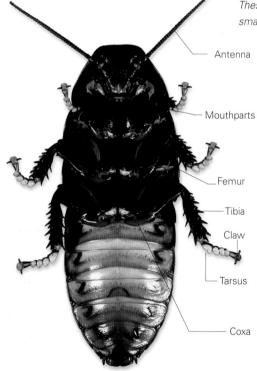

Antenna

Mouthparts

Femur

Tibia

Claw

Tarsus

Coxa

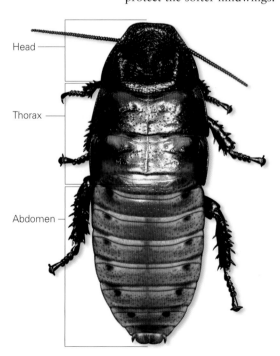

Head

Thorax

Abdomen

Above: The eyes of a damselfly bulge out like beads from the side of its head; giving it almost 360-degree vision. Dragonfly eyes have 30,000 lenses. Most insects have compound eyes made up of many tiny facets.

The abdomen

An insect's abdomen may appear to have fewer segments than are actually present because some may be fused together. The first segment may be reduced or incorporated into the thorax and the eleventh segment may be absent in certain species. The pregenital segments (the first seven abdominal segments) of most adults are similar in arrangement and lack appendages. In many insects, the abdomen is brightly coloured and patterned, often as a warning signal. In others, such as the stick and leaf insects, it has spines or flanges that help protect the insect or conceal it from predators.

The genitalia are formed from modified appendages on segments eight and nine of the abdomen. These appendages are usually small and concealed inside the body, with certain exceptions such as female crickets, which have highly conspicuous ovipositors that they use to lay their eggs deep in soil.

Apart from the ovipositors, the most obvious abdominal appendages are the cerci (paired appendages), which articulate from the last abdominal segment. They are typically long and slender (as in mayflies) but may be modified (for example, the forceps of earwigs). Not all insects possess cerci.

The senses

Insects owe much of their adaptability to their acute senses, especially their ability to sense vibrations, scents and light, including ultraviolet. Many insects have large eyes, providing all-round vision and colour discrimination, used notably by those species that feed from flowers. Some can even detect the plane of polarization of light. In most insects, there is a trade-off between visual acuity and chemical or tactile acuity: those insects with well-developed eyes usually have reduced or simple antennae, and vice-versa. Touch sensors are concentrated on the antennae and legs, but also occur elsewhere on the body. Many insects are very sensitive to vibrations.

In many insects, the sense of taste is well developed and in some, for example the housefly, the taste receptors are found not in the mouth region but on the feet.

There are a variety of different mechanisms by which insects can pick up sound. Crickets' ears occur on their legs and some insects have membranous organs similar to our own eardrums while others have hairs or bristles to detect sound. The range of frequencies insects can hear is often quite narrow. Many insects rely on sound for effective communication.

Insects have also been shown to be able to detect and respond to gravity and the Earth's magnetic field. In summary, insects are mostly highly responsive and often react quickly.

Different antennae

Insects use their antennae as feelers and scent detectors, learning about their surroundings through touch and smell. Those which rely on vision, such as bees, have relatively simple antennae. Those of some beetles are long and used to investigate the area immediately in front of the insect's head. Insects for which smell is important for finding food or mates often have quite complex antennae, adapted to increase the surface area for sensory cells.

Above: Male moths use their feathery antennae to detect the pheromones produced by potential mates.

Above: The antennae of a cockchafer end in leaf-like extensions. Males have seven leaves and females have six.

Below: Some beetles have long, branched antennae.

Below: Insect antennae are composed of many segments as shown below.

INSECT LIFE CYCLES

The vast majority of insects lay eggs: only a few give birth to active young. A tough shell and one or more internal membranes protect these eggs, enabling them to survive a wide range of conditions. A period of dormancy often interrupts the progression from egg to newly hatched larva or nymph.

The wingless insects and some secondarily wingless species are similar in form to the adult when they hatch, but they lack reproductive organs. As the young insect grows up, apart from an increase in size, there is little or no change in its physical appearance.

Winged insects have a more complex development. When the young insect hatches it is often visibly quite different from the adult and must undergo a series of changes before reaching the adult state. This series of changes is known as metamorphosis. Insects possess a tough, non-living external skeleton, which must be shed periodically to enable them to grow in stages. This shedding process is called moulting or ecdysis. Most insects moult between four and ten times. The stages of life between moults are called instars. Newly moulted insects are soft and vulnerable at first.

Partial or incomplete metamorphosis

Winged insects fall into two groups according to the way in which the wings and bodies of the young develop. In the first group, which includes cockroaches, grasshoppers and bugs, the wings of the insect develop gradually on the outside of the body and get larger at each moult until they are fully formed. Nymphs, as the larval insects are usually called at these young stages, often resemble the adult in appearance and behaviour, inhabiting the same places and eating the same types of food. This group, called the Exopterygota in reference to the external development of the wings, are said to undergo a partial (or incomplete) metamorphosis since there are no dramatic changes in body form during development. The young insect gradually changes as it grows, eventually attaining full adult appearance. Some, however, such as lice, are wingless.

Complete metamorphosis

In the second group of winged insects, which includes butterflies, moths, beetles and flies, the young are very different from the adult. Larvae, as the insects of this group are known in the young stages, often occupy a completely different niche and exist on completely different diets from those of the adult. Larvae are generally worm-like in appearance and can be divided into five different forms; eruciform (caterpillar-like), scarabaeiform (grub-like), campodeiform (elongated, flattened and active), elateriform (wireworm-like) and vermiform (maggot-like). The young of this group must undergo one very dramatic change to reach the adult form as opposed to a series of small changes. Because of this, a resting stage is needed, in which the young larva does not feed. This resting stage is the pupa or chrysalis.

The resting phase

There are three types of pupae; obtect (the pupa is compact, with the legs and other appendages enclosed), exarate (the pupa has the legs and other appendages free and extended) and coarctate (the pupa develops inside the larval skin).

Emergence from the pupa

Although most insects need some time for their crumpled wings to open out, certain species of fly such as the mayfly and caddis fly, are able to fly as soon as they emerge from their pupal skins. Those that must wait usually try to find a place that can hold them up, enabling their wings to open out freely. Blood pumped through the veins helps the wings to open out. An insect's

---

Incomplete metamorphosis

Insects which lack wings barely alter in form through their lives after the egg stage. Their moulting stages are classified as incomplete metamorphosis.

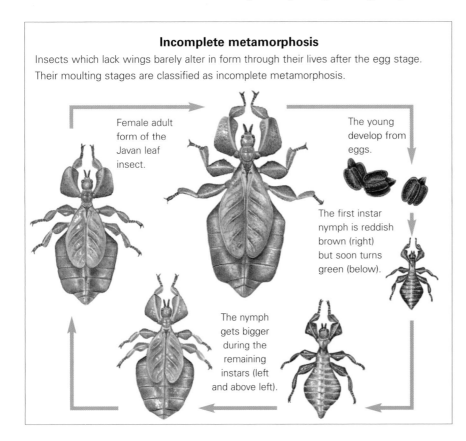

Female adult form of the Javan leaf insect.

The young develop from eggs.

The first instar nymph is reddish brown (right) but soon turns green (below).

The nymph gets bigger during the remaining instars (left and above left).

wings usually need a couple of hours to harden before it is ready to fly. In order for their wings to be ready for flight at a certain time of day, some insect species time their emergence from the pupa very efficiently. Most insects will usually stop growing once the wings are fully developed or when sexual maturity has been reached. A fully developed adult is known as an imago.

Adult life stage

The adult stage has a reproductive role and in insects with relatively inactive larvae, it is often the stage during which they disperse. The adult may be able to reproduce as soon as it has emerged from the pupa or there may be a maturation period before sperm transfer or oviposition can occur. The number of reproductive cycles an adult insect has is dependent upon the species and food availability. It can range between one and many. The adults of certain species are very short-lived, for example, mayflies, midges and male scale insects. They fly for only a few hours, or at the most a day or two, before dying. They need to mate within this time. Most adult insects live for a few weeks or months and some are particularly long-lived – queen bees and ants, and queen termites, for instance. Many large, winged insects, such as butterflies, may fly long distances, even migrating to regions with a more favourable climate before reproducing. Many also hibernate to survive the winter, often in the pupal stage, emerging when food is available the next season.

Above: A dragonfly perches next to its empty larval skin. Dragonfly larvae live in water and must climb out before they can break free from their skin and emerge as adults. These ghost-like empty cases may be found clinging to waterside stems.

Complete metamorphosis

Butterflies undergo complete metamorphosis. Their bodies and habits change dramatically from the many-legged caterpillar borne of the egg, to the winged adult form, via a 'resting' pupa (chrysalis) stage, which may last for weeks.

1 *A butterfly egg waits to hatch. Butterflies lay on the stems or leaves of plants on which their caterpillars feed.*

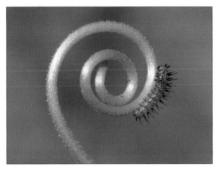

2 *The newly hatched caterpillar is small but completely independent. Its job now is to feed and grow.*

3 *As the caterpillar grows it changes colour. The bright yellow indicates that it is unpleasant to eat.*

4 *After several weeks of feeding the caterpillar has grown to hundreds of times its original size. It is now ready for metamorphosis.*

5 *Following a week or more as a pupa the adult butterfly emerges from its chrysalis (case). Next it will unfurl its wings and pump them up with blood.*

6 *After extending and drying its fully formed wings for several hours, this butterfly can take to the air and search for a mate and food.*

INSECT FLIGHT

The insects are the only group of invertebrates to have developed flight. This development has allowed insects greater mobility, which helps enormously when searching for food and mates. This ability has also allowed insects to exploit many new environments and habitats.

Insects began flying 350 million years ago. The earliest flying insects had two sets of wings, and were unable to fold them over their abdomen. Most insects today have either one pair of wings or two pairs functioning as a single pair. Natural selection has played a huge role in refining the wings, and the control and sensory systems, as well as everything else that affects aerodynamics and movement through the air. One significant trait is wing twist. Most insect wings are twisted, between 10 and 20 degrees, giving them a higher angle relative to the ground at the base. As well as this, the wing membrane is distorted and angled between the veins in such a way that the cross-section of the wing acts as an airfoil. The wing's basic shape is therefore very efficient at producing lift.

Below: Dragonflies have two pairs of long, rather rigid, membranous wings. Unlike their smaller relatives, the damselflies, they hold their wings open when at rest (damselflies close their wings over their long abdomens).

Most insects use tiny muscles in the thorax to adjust the tilt, stiffness and flapping frequency of the wings, thus keeping them in control. The capabilities of flying insects vary but some are able to hover and even fly backward.

Take-off
In order to fly, an insect must overcome the forces of gravity and air resistance to movement. In gliding flight, in which the wings are held rigidly outstretched, the use of passive air movements helps overcome these forces. By adjusting the angle of the leading edge of the wing when orientated into the wind, an insect achieves lift. As this angle (the angle of attack) increases, lift also increases. The angle of attack of insects can be raised to more than 30 degrees, giving them great manoeuvrability. There are two considerably different insect flight mechanisms, and each has its own advantages and disadvantages. Most insects glide; some a little, for example the flies (Diptera), and some a lot, for instance the dragonflies (Odonata).

Above: Grasshoppers and locusts only have fully formed wings as adults. When immature nymphs, as here, their wings are visible but only partially formed and useless for flight. Their enlarged legs provide the power for leaping instead.

Getting airborne: method one
It is by beating their wings that most winged insects fly. A single wing beat comprises three interlinked movements. The first is a sequence of downward, forward movements followed by upward and backward movements using the whole wing, fully extended. Second, during the sequence each wing is rotated around its base for extra manoeuvrability. Third, in response to local variations in air pressure, various parts of the wing flex. In true flight, the movement of the wings produces the relative wind whereas in gliding it comes from passive air movement.

Wing muscles
The different flight mechanisms used by flying insects are brought about by two kinds of arrangements of muscles powering their flight. These are: direct flight muscles connected to the wings, and indirect muscle action, whereby internal body muscles cause wing movements by changing the shape of the thorax. The wings have rubber-like hinges that add extra elasticity.

Above: Butterflies and moths have wings covered with numerous tiny scales – it is these which give them their colour and pattern. The wings of butterflies and moths are the largest of any insects relative to body size.

Getting airborne: method two

Unlike those of most other insects, the wing muscles of insects belonging to the orders Odonata (the dragonflies and damselflies) and Blattodea (the cockroaches) insert directly at the wing bases, which are hinged so that a small movement of the wing base downward lifts the wing itself upward. In mayflies, the hind wings are reduced, sometimes absent, and play little role in their flight. The primitive flight mechanism of the Odonata and Blattodea does not necessarily mean they are poorer fliers. More advanced insects use indirect muscles for flight. However, they do also retain direct muscles which are used for making fine adjustments to wing orientation during flight. When the muscles attached to the wing base inside the pivotal point contract, an upward stroke is produced. When the muscles that extend from the sternum (the upper half of the exoskeleton) to the wing base outside the pivot point contract, a downward stroke is produced. These are direct flight muscle movements. The indirect flight muscles are attached to the tergum (the lower half of the exoskeleton) and the sternum. The tergum connects to the base of the wing. When the vertical muscles inside the thorax contract, the tergum is pulled down, thus raising the wings in the upstroke, and stretching the horizontal muscles. When the horizontal muscles contract, the wings are lowered in the down-stroke, stretching the vertical muscles.

Synchronized wings

Although the beating of the wings may be controlled independently, it is more common for them to be harmonized, as in butterflies, bugs and bees, for example. This is accomplished by locking the fore- and hindwings together and also through neural control, synchronizing the nerve patterns going to each from the brain. Insects that have slower wing-beat frequencies (for example, dragonflies) possess synchronous muscles, which help to maintain one nerve impulse for each beat. Insects with faster beating wings (such as wasps, flies and beetles) have asynchronous muscles whereby a single nerve impulse causes a muscle fibre to contract multiple times allowing the frequency of wing-beats to exceed the rate at which the nervous system can send impulses. Some small flies can flap their wings at more than 1,000 times per second.

As well as powered flight, many of the world's smaller insects are dispersed on the wind. For example, aphids are often transported long distances by low-level jet-stream winds and many migrant species make use of prevailing winds and air currents.

Below: Hoverflies are master fliers. As their name suggests, they can stay in one spot in midair. They can also fly backward. It is the venation in the wings that allows the species to be told apart from bees and wasps, all of which are common visitors to garden flowers.

INSECT SOCIAL ORGANIZATION

The vast majority of insect species are solitary. Any interaction within these species is usually confined to mating or competition. However, some insects spend their whole lives in huge colonies, while others gather together in large numbers at certain times of the year.

Bees, some wasps, ants and termites are all social insects, living in caste systems. Their social organization is known as eusociality. Other insects such as beetles, cockroaches, bugs, butterflies, hymenopterans and thysanopterans have less developed social habits and group together for specific reasons. Their social interaction is known as subsocial.

Eusocial insects

In a caste system there is a clearly defined division of labour among members. The members co-operate in order to ensure the life of the colony. Many sterile members of a colony care for a few reproductive members. The sterile members carry out specialized tasks, such as feeding reproductive members and caring for the young. Workers maintain the hive and defend it from attack. An overlap of generations assists the functioning of the colony.

Caste systems

The caste system is made up of one or several reproductive individuals called queens who are aided by the numerous non-reproductive workers. In termite

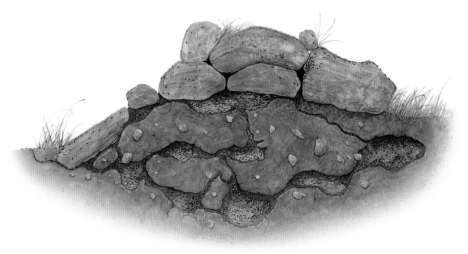

Above: Areas beneath surface stones are often chosen for ants' nests as they soak up the sun's warmth by day and radiate it out at night.

and ant colonies there is often an additional defensive group of individuals called soldiers. In some species the queens and soldiers are unable to feed themselves and it is the job of the workers to bring them food.

In eusocial hymenopterans the queens control the sex of their offspring by fertilizing the eggs with stored sperm. These eggs then develop into diploid females. These sisters are more related to each other than queens are to their offspring, sharing 75 per cent of their genes on average. Male offspring are produced when eggs are unfertilized. The production of males is infrequent and they die after mating.

The queen of a colony is generally larger than any worker and has an extended abdomen. In her first brood, she will only produce workers. Once these have hatched she will cease to forage and devote herself entirely to reproduction. The workers carry out tasks such as foraging and food distribution, cleaning, ventilating and guarding the nest.

In an ant colony there are two major female castes, the queen and the workers, which usually look completely different. Some ant workers are divided into subcastes known as minor, media or major, according to their size. In contrast to the female-only castes of the eusocial hymenoptera, termite castes include both male and female representatives. All termite colonies have a king as well as a queen who act as the primary reproductives. The workers and soldiers in ant colonies also consist of males and females. The colonies of some termites are huge, with up to a million individuals.

Below: Many ant species build their nests underground, excavating numerous chambers. An entrance is shown here.

Below: Unlike most ants, termites are exclusively herbivorous insects, eating only plant matter. They are particularly common in grassland habitats, where they tend to live in mounds. This is a queen termite.

Subsocial insects

Insects with subsocial habits are more common than those with eusocial habits. An example of a subsocial interaction is the non-reproductive gathering of monarch butterflies at overwintering sites in Mexico and California. Many tropical butterflies gather together to roost in safety, particularly those species that have warning coloration on their bodies, or odours and an unpleasant taste. A solitary insect of this kind is more at risk of being predated upon than a single member of a conspicuous group.

Parental roles

Among subsocial insects, parents do take care of their young. For those insects that do not nest, it is predominantly the adult female that attends to the eggs and early instars, although paternal guarding is known in some tropical assassin bugs and giant water bugs. The parent protects the eggs against parasitization and predation, keeping eggs free from fungi and maintaining the correct conditions for egg development.

Nesting

Only five social insect orders build nests in which to reproduce, four of which are subsocial and one that is eusocial. Insects such as earwigs and mole crickets, which are solitary insects, exhibit similar parental care. After overwintering together in the same nest, the female of the species ejects the male in the spring as she begins to tend to her eggs.

Below: Queen bees are larger than the male bees, or drones, which, in turn, are larger than the workers.

queen

male

worker

Above: A termite mound is a complex structure built from soil particles held together with sticky saliva. The large central chamber acts like a chimney, so that air is drawn in at the bottom, ventilating the mound.

Among dung and carrion beetles, there is competition for nutrient-rich dung in which to lay eggs. The female is mainly responsible for burrowing and preparing the dung, which is sometimes rolled away from its source or else coated in clay. Some species of beetle take no further interest in the eggs once they have been laid.

Subsocial parasitoid wasps, which attack and immobilize arthropod prey upon which their young feed, exhibit numerous prey-handling and nesting strategies that can be quite complex. Some use the prey's own burrow for nesting while others either build a simple burrow after prey is captured or make their nest burrow before they capture their prey.

Parental care with communal nesting most commonly occurs among subsocial bees and wasps. The females of these species remain in the nest after laying and often until the next generation have emerged as adults. They maintain nest hygiene by removing faeces and guard the nest against specialized nest parasites.

Above: Tropical butterflies with distasteful flesh often roost together. Although most carry warning colours for potential predators, these are enhanced and the effect amplified by the insects' occurrence in groups.

Some aphids have a soldier caste in which some first- or second-instar nymphs never develop into adults. These nymphs exhibit aggressive behaviour and are physically modified so that they are larger than non-soldier nymphs. Using either their frontal horns or their mouthparts as piercing weapons, they attack intruders and protect the aphid colony. Potter wasps make neat cup-shaped cells of mud, each containing a paralysed prey and an egg laid by the wasp.

Below: Termite queens are so large that they are unable to move much. They rely entirely on the other members of the colony for survival.

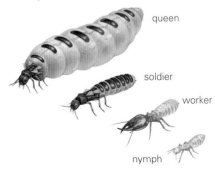

queen

soldier

worker

nymph

INSECT DEFENCES

Insects use a range of defence mechanisms, and for a variety of reasons. They may be used to ward off competition during mating and feeding, or to avoid or deal with predators. Mimicry, chemicals, weapons and camouflage comprise some of an insect's arsenal, often coupled with specialized behaviour.

An insect's in-built weaponry includes stings, biting mouthparts and adapted claws for nipping. An insect's sting evolved with the specific purpose of delivering venom. In the case of bees, using the sting leads to the insect's death, as crucial parts of organs are removed as the sting is torn away. Bees sting to defend their colonies from attack by large predators.

Some insects, such as those with adapted claws or mandibles, indulge in ritualized fighting, which avoids real harm to either party. The impressive mandibles of the male stag beetle *Lucanus cervus* are used as an indication of strength and to wrestle opponents (unlike the nipping mouthparts of the smaller female of the species).

Speed as defence

The ability to react swiftly and move away quickly is a good form of defence. Ground beetles can run fast, while winged insects such as flies and dragonflies can fly away from danger and are also equipped with excellent vision. Other forms of locomotion for escape include physical propulsion, as in the click beetles, which, due to a mobile joint in the thorax, can flick themselves high into the air. Click beetles make a loud noise when

Above: A tough, spiky carapace offers protection from some predators, although it is not always effective against larger creatures, such as birds.

Above: Powerful mandibles can give a nasty nip. Perhaps surprisingly, short mandibles like these bite with more force than longer ones.

flipping themselves, which may also be used as an alarm to distract or confuse enemies. Grasshoppers and crickets have excellent strong jumping legs, as do fleas, which can jump great distances relative to their size.

Swift movements combined with a flash of bright coloration can also confuse a predator. Some tropical locusts have brightly coloured wing patches which they flash at their predators as they flee from them. If the bright colour is only viewed briefly and the insect swiftly drops into grass, the predator will try to follow the

insect in the direction of the flash, which tends to guide it away from the potential prey hidden safely below. Conversely, staying still can also be an effective defence. Fierce, predatory mantids will tend to overlook a motionless insect, not recognizing it as prey.

Warning colours

Some insects use the toxic qualities of their food to generate similar compounds within themselves and thus become unpalatable to predators. They advertise the fact that they taste bad (or are toxic) by using bright warning colours such as red, black and yellow on their body parts. The black and yellow striped cinnabar moth caterpillar which feeds on ragwort, a plant poisonous to many other animals, is just one example of an insect which does this. Insects generating their own chemical protection often group together to

Left: Although it looks dangerous, the male scorpion fly's 'sting' is actually fake. It is thought that the fly mimics a scorpion's sting for protection from predators.

increase the effect of this defence should they come under attack. Parasites of such insects may also utilize these chemicals further for their own defences.

Mimicry

Many non-poisonous and harmless insect species mimic the warning coloration and patterns of more dangerous ones to take advantage of the effects of the predators' learned response to those creatures without having to eat the food plant or synthesize chemicals themselves. To be convincing, these mimic insects also adopt the postures of the species they are pretending to be. Thus the European bee beetle (*Trichius fasciatus*) mimics bumblebees (such as *Bombus lucorum*) by appearing to feed on flower-heads in the same way as a bumblebee (plunging its whole body into the pollen of composite flowers). It also has a large yellow-and-black body with hairs on and around its elytra. Its general bulk and appearance is similar to a bee when glimpsed in flight.

However, it is not as convincing as some of the clearwing moths, from the family Sesiidae, for instance, which mimic the appearance of paper wasps. They are active in the daytime and move in the same way as the wasps. Another mimic is the European bee fly *Bombylius major,* which looks rather like a fluffy bee with its hairy round abdomen.

The male scorpion fly, on the other hand, superficially resembles a scorpion. It has a bulbous projection on the end of its abdomen, which it curls up like a scorpion's sting to ward off predators.

Chemical warfare

Many other insects use chemicals as defence. These are often produced within the insect iself, sometimes by eating particular food plants. Chemicals are synthesized by the insects internally to squirt or inflict on enemies by a variety of methods. Particularly noxious chemicals are thought to be made swiftly on demand

Above: Bright colours and bold patterns are used by many insects to warn predators that they are poisonous or taste bad.

to reduce any toxic effects on the insect's own body. The bombardier beetle (*Brachinus crepitans*) dramatically produces a blister-forming volatile liquid, which is squirted from its abdomen. This quickly turns to gas with a dramatic pop to ward off unwanted attention. Many ants squirt formic acid, and worker termites are capable of squirting noxious secretions from specialized head glands to ward off predators. Stink bugs gained their common name from their ability to release a foul-smelling fluid from special glands when alarmed. Sometimes defence mechanisms combine and mimics may even go as far as producing identical chemical defences to those of the insect they mimic (as in the case of ant mimics).

Alarm pheromones are chemicals synthesized within an insect and which are used to communicate danger to other insects of the same species. They act by triggering an immediate response from the recipient of the chemical message. Such chemicals are highly specific and even very similar molecules create a different reaction. Alarm pheromones take effect quickly then soon fade away after their task

has been accomplished. Interestingly this method is also used by predatory insects, which in effect raise a false alarm. By releasing massive quantities of simulated alarm pheromone an invading species is able to attack a colony under the cover of the almost certain chaos the false alarm will create.

Social defence mechanisms

Termites and ants have developed co-operative social responses to defending vulnerable offspring, using armoured soldiers that repel invaders of their colonies. Hard chitinous processes have evolved to provide weapons on the specially adapted heads of soldiers and, among ants, strong biting jaws also dissuade hungry visitors. In soldier termites the jaws are purely for defence. Their fellow workers feed them as they do not search for food themselves.

Certain species of honey bee have been shown to co-operate in defending their hives by attacking enemies as a group. Where their stings are unable to penetrate the hard surface of a hornet, for example, attacking their nest, the honey bees have been observed surrounding the enemy until it is completely smothered by many individuals. In some cases, the intruder is killed through suffocation or even by the heat generated by the mass of attacking bees.

Below: Camouflage is used by some insects to hide from both predators and prey. This praying mantis has a wide, flat carapace which helps disguise it as a leaf.

INSECT CAMOUFLAGE

Most insects are vulnerable to attack from a wide range of predators. Camouflage is one of their favoured methods of escaping detection and many insects closely resemble their backgrounds, some having strange spines or projections to enhance this effect.

Many insects display cryptic coloration, whereby their body colour is used to help them blend into the background and effectively disappear from view. Cryptic coloration indicates that an insect is well adapted to the habitat or niche in which it lives. It allows an insect to become part of its immediate background – a plant or other surface. It is an approach used both by predators who lie in wait, and by potential prey species trying to avoid being eaten by making themselves less conspicuous to the creatures which hunt them.

Many moths rest by day against the bark of trees and can then be extremely hard to spot. Some have cryptic patterns on their upper wings. Butterflies that are brightly coloured on the upperside frequently have well-camouflaged underwings. Red admirals and peacock butterflies, for example, can be very hard to see when at rest or when hibernating with their wings closed, as their hindwings are brown, and speckled and patterned like bark.

Below: Many crickets hunt from leaves. Most mimic leaf colour and texture well, being green and brown.

Above: Most moths rest by day and are beautifully camouflaged. The true number of moths around us is often under-estimated, as they are so difficult to see.

Chameleon insects

Some species have the ability to change colour with seasonal changes in their environment. Predatory African mantid species, for example, can be very green in the wet season in the presence of lush vegetation but change to a brown coloration during the dry season when most of the vegetation has dried out and died back. In Australia, a similar mechanism, known as fire melanism, occurs whereby Australian mantid species are able to camouflage themselves in the black landscape that appears after a bush fire.

Melanism also occurs in the cryptic camouflage of the peppered moth (*Biston betularia*), which closely resembles the pattern and colours of the tree bark on which it rests. As far back as the 19th century it was noted that moths resting on blackened surfaces resulting from industrial pollution tended to be darker than those found in less polluted areas, where the tree trunks had a lighter covering caused by active growth of lichens. In this case, predation by birds removed more of the less well-camouflaged moths in each area.

Body shape

Insect exoskeletons vary in shape and provide a disguise with another dimension, as in the case of leaf and stick insects. They enable insects to take on not only the colour of their surroundings but also the shape of objects in it. Many mantids also have bodies resembling parts of plants, with very convincing leaf-like or petal-like projections or textures. Stick and leaf

Below: When at rest, orthopterans often pass unnoticed. They are recognizable by their large hind legs, adapted for jumping.

insects provide very convincing imitations of twigs and leaves, even swaying to resemble foliage in the breeze. They also assume a pose with their front legs facing forward in line with the twig they are emulating. Mantids, too, often sway gently from side to side in order to match the movements of the leaves or flowers on which they sit.

Imitation

Insect eggs often closely resemble plant seeds and are dropped to ground level or glued to plant leaves. Those at ground level may be carried away by ants mistaking them for seeds. Young stick insects hatching in ant nests suffer less predation than those left in the open, so this helps their survival. The small dark young quickly travel upward once hatched to the relative safety of the underside of a leaf until, after a few moults, they too take on the colour and camouflage of the host plant. Stick insects, as well as camouflaging themselves to resemble plants, try to make their overall presence less obvious by propelling their droppings beyond food plants with some vigour. This avoids obvious signs of their presence.

Patterns and textures of mimics, though very convincing, will often also involve behaviour that enhances their effect, such as the closed-wing posture of the Indian leaf butterfly (*Kallima*

Left: A slender mantis hides very well on the delicate stem of a flower.

inachus) whose wing undersides are shaped and patterned to appear similar to the fallen leaves it perches among. When this butterfly opens its wings it becomes much more obvious, due to the bright colours of its upper wings. Some caterpillars appear very like the twigs of their food plants and adopt an angled posture on a twig, often causing them to be overlooked.

The colours and patterning of cryptic insects and plant or habitat mimics are designed to help them blend in with the backgrounds of the places where they live. However, these insects may have hidden areas of bright colour, which they flash to startle predators when they find themselves attacked. An insect such as a stick insect or cricket may suddenly take flight to avoid danger and as it does so it will display normally hidden wing patches or bright areas on legs. This serves to shock the predator, stopping it in its tracks and giving the insect time to make an attempt at escape. It may also confuse the predator into losing the trail of its prey. Flash coloration can also take the form of false eye markings, as on the normally hidden wings of the

Below: This scorpion has coloration that blends well with the gravel background on which it is resting.

Above: This mantis blends into its background seamlessly.

otherwise cryptic peanut-headed bug (*Fulgora laternaria*). These markings are at the opposite end to its actual head, which also aids its survival, as predators often strike at the head when attacking.

It is possible that there are forms of camouflage in nature that human eyes do not register, since we see a different range of wavelengths from insects. In ultraviolet light, for example, other patterns may be revealed.

Below: This leaf insect gives the appearance of a dead leaf. Its colouring helps to camouflage it from predators.

INSECT FEEDING METHODS

Insects generally have two methods of feeding. They either bite off and chew their food or they drink it in liquid form. The types of food consumed by different insect groups are many and varied. They include sap, leaves, vertebrate blood, dry wood, bacteria and algae, and the internal tissues of other insects.

Insects have various different mouthparts, which correlate with the sort of diet they have. For example, termites have tough biting jaws with which they feed on wood, and butterflies have a long proboscis with which they suck nectar from flowers. The gut structure and function of each insect family varies too depending on the nutrient composition of the food they eat. Insects that eat solid food have a broad, straight, short gut, while liquid-feeding insects have a longer, narrower gut that allows more contact with the ingested liquid.

Feeding categories

Insects generally specialize in one of four different feeding categories, depending on whether the food they eat is solid or liquid, or from a plant or an animal source. However, those with a more generalized diet will fall between two or more of these categories, for example bees feed both on pollen (a plant solid) and nectar (a plant liquid), and most endopterygotes (insects with larval stages) will change from one category to another depending on their life stage (for

Below: Moths and butterflies suck liquid food from plants by means of a proboscis which is coiled out of the way until needed.

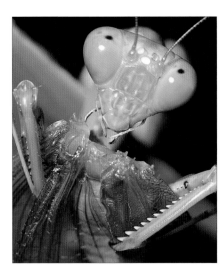

Above: A praying mantis feeds on prey. Its mouthparts are small but sharp, for slicing flesh.

Above: Bumblebees have both a long 'tongue' for collecting nectar and mandibles for crushing pollen.

instance moths and butterflies switch from a diet of leaves as larvae to a diet of nectar as adults).

Mandibulates

Insects that bite and chew their food are known as mandibulates. Examples of these include cockroaches, crickets and earwigs. The mouthparts of these insects are the more basic design and are composed of five main parts. The mandibles (or jaws), which can be extremely hard, help to cut and grind food. They do this with tooth-like

ridges for cutting, and crushing surfaces for grinding. The maxillae lie behind the mandibles and assist them in processing food. The maxillary palp is found behind the maxillae and bears sensory hairs. The upper lip forms the roof of the preoral cavity and mouth, while the lower lip forms the floor of the preoral cavity. The labium has one pair of palps also bearing mechano-receptors. The final mouthpart is a tongue-like structure which divides the preoral cavity into a dorsal food pouch and a ventral salivarium from which saliva enters the mouth.

Haustellates

Evolution has led to the development of an array of different mouthpart types. There has been such diversification in different orders that in addition to the basic chewing method, lapping, sucking, biting, piercing and filter-feeding are all also employed by various species. Bees use

Left: Blister beetles are voracious feeders, contaminating animal feed crops with toxins at the same time.

their mouthparts for both chewing and lapping. Lapping occurs when an insect uses a protrusible organ to acquire a liquid or semi-liquid food, which is then transferred to the mouth. The honey bee, *Apis mellifera*, does this by dipping its hair-covered tongue into nectar or honey, which sticks to the hairs and is then retracted and carried up the bee's food canal.

Insects that obtain their food solely by sucking up liquids are called haustellates. Most moths and butterflies, and many adult flies fall into this category. The sucking mouthparts of these insects are elongated. Muscles help pump the liquid food. The proboscis of moths and butterflies is loosely coiled until the insect wishes to feed, whereupon it is extended. The upper surface of the proboscis is more or less flat when coiled, but contraction of the muscles causes the upper surface to become slightly domed, which automatically causes the proboscis to uncoil.

Combination feeders

A combination of sucking with either piercing or biting is used by a few moths and many flies. For example, bloodsucking flies such as mosquitoes and horseflies possess sharp, piercing mandibles and maxillae. Lobes carried on the tip of the labium or proboscis, are used to suck up the liquid food after piercing. In contrast, tsetse flies

Below: Leaf cutter ants return to their colony. These ants use leaf sections to grow fungi, on which they feed.

Differing mouthparts

As a group, insects have incredibly varied mouthparts, although in most these are formed from the same basic components: the mandibles, the maxillary palps, the labrum and the labium. Most insects either lap up food, crush or chew it, or suck it up through a tube. In the latter, the tube like mouthparts can either be stiff for piercing or flexible for probing.

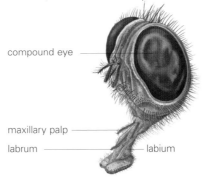

compound eye — maxillary palp — labrum — labium

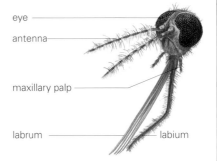

eye — antenna — maxillary palp — labrum — labium

Above: A fly's mouthparts are adapted for lapping up tiny particles or liquid food.

Above: The female mosquito feeds on the blood of mammals and other large animals.

Below: Predatory beetles have long spiked mandibles for grabbing prey.

Below: The tube like mouthparts of butterflies are adapted for sucking up nectar.

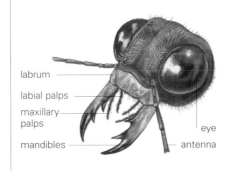

labrum — labial palps — maxillary palps — mandibles — eye — antenna

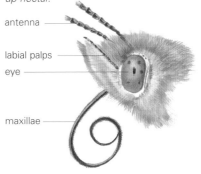

antenna — labial palps — eye — maxillae

---

and stable flies use their highly modified labium for piercing.

True bugs, thrips, fleas and sucking lice have modified mouthparts for sucking and piercing. The labium of nymphal damselflies and dragonflies is

uniquely modified. This mask-like structure is hinged and can be folded so that it covers most of the underside of the head. Some insects are filter-feeders (for example larval mosquitoes, black flies and caddis flies) and obtain their food by filtering particles from the water in which they live. This food includes bacteria, microscopic algae and detritus. The mouthparts of such filter-feeders include a number of setal 'brushes' or 'fans' which generate feeding currents or trap tiny food particles and move them to the mouth.

The mouthparts of some adult insects, such as mayflies and warble flies, are greatly reduced and non-functional.

Left: Mosquitoes use their sharp mouthparts to pierce flesh and suck blood.

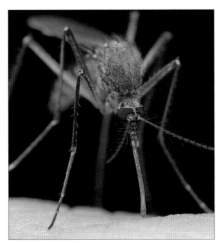

USEFUL INSECTS

Among the vast range of insects alive today there are many that are useful to people, notably as pollinators of crops that humans eat. Honey bees also produce honey and wax. Many insects are beneficial to the gardener, killing insect pests.

Insects, especially bees, butterflies, flies and moths, play a valuable role in the pollination of flowering plants. This is of economic importance for some crops and of vital importance for food chains and webs.

Insects break down matter at the lower end of the food chain, improving soil quality by affecting its structure and fertility. This in turn aids the plants that grow in it and benefits everything up the food chain. The effects of insects recycling decaying matter in rainforests may be as important as the effect of worms on the soil structure in such habitats.

Beneficial bees

Some insects provide us with food. Honey is the delicious and nutritious liquid we harvest from honey-bee hives. This practice has gone on for centuries, honey often being collected from wild bee nests by native people or cultivated by providing hives for bees and in effect farming them.

Wax is a another natural product derived from beehives and people have found many uses for its numerous qualities. It burns (making it a useful alternative to oil and tallow), melts and acts as a sealant (for dyeing processes such as batik), and is used as a traditional material in woodworking and crafts (as a wood sealant or lubricant), as well as being added to some skin products.

In the realms of alternative medicine, bees also figure prominently. Propolis is a substance synthesized in beehives as part of bees' own natural defences to bacteria. It is made available to humans in the form of a herbal remedy for coughs and sore throats and thought generally to boost immunity. Herbal medicines also use royal jelly (made to feed the queen bee larvae) as a health supplement. Many alternative health practitioners believe that eating a locally produced honey will help some individuals who suffer from hay fever to overcome their allergy, as a result of exposure to a product derived from local pollen.

Nutritious foodstuff

Whole insects are consumed by some indigenous people as part of their normal diet, being considered both tasty and nutritious, due to their high protein content. In Africa some people collect midges and squash them into a

Above: Dung beetles help keep the African savanna clean, collecting dung and making it into balls in which they lay their eggs.

flat patty to eat when they appear in huge numbers at certain times. The abundance of locusts means they too are often caught (and sometimes cooked) as an easily available meal in a number of places around the globe. In parts of Asia the nymphs of dragonflies are caught and fried like fish, and even the larvae of some tropical wasps are eaten.

In recent times people have come to value the role of insects in the wider food web. Various companies now tempt an increasingly conservation-minded public with a variety of insect-studded bird foods and larvae for the garden bird table as part of supplementary all-year-round feeding.

Beneficial insects

Cochineal insects (*Dactylopius coccus*) have been gathered for at least the past 500 years to produce a red dye (derived from the carminic acid they contain) still used in some cooking and dye products today.

Left: Honey bees are perhaps the most useful of all insects to humans. They not only pollinate crops but also make honey, beeswax and other products we use.

Insects are increasingly being researched and used as biological control agents to deal with outbreaks of species threatening to affect crops or plant collections. These are alternatives to chemically derived and often non-specific pesticides, and they are increasingly being seen as an organic alternative to more destructive chemical approaches. A predatory insect species is introduced to deal with outbreaks of 'harmful' insect species that may otherwise destroy the plants. One example is the tiny hymenopteran parasitic wasp (*Encarsia formosa*) which is introduced to plants to eliminate whitefly *Trialeurodes vaporariorum* (actually a member of the bug order). *Encarsia* acts by feeding on the nymph stages of the bug.

Since 1200BC, shellac has been derived from insects (notably from the hemipteran *Kerria lacca*) for varied uses including varnish, food and hair dye. Shellac is still economically important enough to be harvested in India, Thailand and China, and is used in jewellery and ornaments as well as the aforementioned products.

Forensic science

Forensic entomology is a useful if somewhat unusual application of the study of insects which can provide crucial evidence in unsolved murder

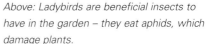

Above: Ladybirds are beneficial insects to have in the garden – they eat aphids, which damage plants.

cases. An in-depth knowledge of fly species (Diptera) is often used, especially the larval stages or maggots which may be found on a corpse. By analysing details of the stage of the life cycle relative to the species observed, estimations can be made of the actual time of death of a victim when no other evidence is available. Clues for reconstructing a crime scene may result.

We have made use of our knowledge of insect pheromones by synthesizing them to place in traps to act as insect lures. Pests can be captured before they get the chance to raid or contaminate food (for example cockroaches or beetles in grain stores). Traps have also

found an unexpected use in museums, helping to protect antiquities and precious items made from natural fibres which are attacked by dermestid beetles. One such pest is so prevalent that it has become known as the 'museum beetle' due to the problems it has caused in collections it perceives as edible. Traps are set in a similar way to those for food store pests, particularly at certain times of year when the beetles may be more mobile than normal, flying some distance to find mates and lay their eggs.

Insect sex pheromones are also used by humans to interrupt mating cycles where a species causes considerable harm to economically important crops. Artificially created sex pheromones are used to fool a species into believing mating is imminent before the crops break through the soil, thus saving the crop from insect damage.

One example of a species being dealt with in this way is the pink bollworm moth (*Pectinophora gossypiella*) which causes damage to cotton crops in the USA, Pakistan and Egypt. Pheromone traps are used, as is biological control using a parasitic wasp.

Below: Flies are often perceived to be pests, but may be useful to criminologists.

THE INSECT ORDERS

There are 30 orders of insect included within the class Insecta. These range from tiny microscopic creatures to tropical stick insects that can measure up to 30cm (12in), and beetles with a similar wingspan. Many of these insects are around us in our homes and gardens and will be familiar creatures.

This chapter provides a brief look at the insects that are included within each order and describes their typical features. The general appearance of each insect group is detailed, with dimensions, body shape and colouring all described. Aspects such as feeding, defence, reproduction and characteristic behaviour are also covered. The life cycle of each insect type is explained, together with any identifying features for each life stage. Finally information is provided about the type of habitat in which typical members of the group are found. Some insects are cosmopolitan, while others have very specific requirements, with a need to be near water, or in damp leaf litter, for example.

Included too are spiders and relatives, millipedes and centipedes, and the wingless near-insects. These groups, like the insects themselves, are (mainly terrestrial) arthropods; they are sometimes confused with insects and may be found in similar habitats.

Left: A damselfly coming in to land shows the net-veined, transparent wings typical of many flying insects. Damselflies are recognizable by their long tapering bodies, which are usually brightly coloured.

WINGLESS NEAR-INSECTS
AND WINGLESS INSECTS

The orders Collembola, Diplura and Protura make up the wingless near-insects. These small arthropods have six legs, and simple mouthparts that are enclosed inside a cavity. The wingless true insects are the bristletails and silverfish (Archaeognatha and Thysanura).

Springtails (Collembola)

These wingless insects are one of the most successful groups of hexapods and are found in amazing numbers. Commonly known as springtails, they range in size from 0.2–10mm (0.01–0.39in).

The name 'springtail' refers to the furcula, a specially adapted appendage underneath the abdomen (not present in all species). It is held in place by a catch. When this is released the furcula will spring back suddenly, launching the animal into the air. Collembolans can be identified by the fact that they have six abdominal segments, four antennal segments, four leg segments and lack terminal cerci. The 6,000 living species of springtail are divided

Above: Diplurans are primitive insects that are wingless and not easy to spot.

into three suborders: the elongate bodies (Arthropleona) containing two superfamilies; and the globular bodies, divided into Neelipleona, which has one family, and Symphypleona, which contains five superfamilies.

Above: Springtails can leap by releasing a powerful spring underneath their bodies.

Reproduction is indirect, with a spermatophore deposited by the male and either left for the female to pick up or placed in her genital opening. The eggs hatch into nymphs that only differ from the adults in size and lack sexual maturity. These nymphs undergo five to eight instar moults, but once adult they continue moulting. Depending on the species, springtails may produce one generation or several. In a lifetime (12 months) a female may lay 90–150 eggs.

The arctic species, *Cryptopygus antarcticus* can tolerate temperatures as low as -60°C (-76°F).

Diplura

The name diplura is derived from 'diploos' (double) and 'oura' (tail), referring to the cerci. Diplurans are slender and small, 2–5mm (0.08–0.19in) long, eyeless and mostly white, with long slender antennae, biting mouthparts and two prominent cerci that are either short and forceps-shaped or long and thread-like.

There are 800 species in nine families. Diplurans may be either herbivorous or carnivorous (predacious hunters), using their pincers to catch prey. The lifespan is approximately one year. Reproduction involves the males leaving spermatophores for females to

---

Life cycle of a springtail

The Lucerne flea, *Sminthurus viridis*, is a primitive wingless insect, whose young look like miniature versions of the adult, once free of the egg.

The female walks over the spermatophore and it comes into contact with her genital opening.

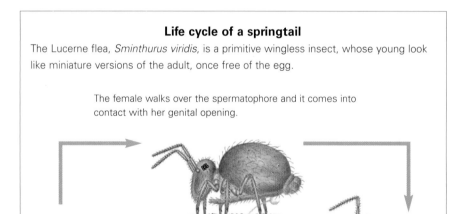

A spermatophore is deposited by the adult male.

Eggs occur in batches.

Young nymphs resemble the adult, except in size.

Newly hatched nymphs are pale yellow.

collect. Their life cycle is simple. The eggs, which are laid in burrows, hatch into nymphs that resemble small adults but lack reproductive organs. Moulting occurs both in the nymphs and adults and may take place over 30 times in a lifetime.

Diplurans can regenerate a lost appendage and may drop their cerci when under attack.

Protura

Less than 2mm (0.08in) long, eyeless and lacking antennae, proturans hold their enlarged front legs forward antennae-like and have sensory abilities. They also lack cerci. The cylindrical abdomen has 12 segments and the legs have five segments.

Between four and eight families have been recognized, with about 500 species described to date.

The more long-legged species appear to have one generation a year, as opposed to the shorter-legged species, which tend to reproduce continuously all year round. Little is known about their reproductive processes, but it is believed that from the egg they have five stages before adult: a pre-larva, two larval types, a junior stage, and a pre-imago (pre-adult).

Habitats of wingless near-insects and wingless insects

Up to 200,000 springtails can live in a single square metre/yard of land, depending on the habitat. Springtails are found from mountain-tops to seashores, and occur on all of the world's continents including Antarctica. The majority of species inhabit leaf litter or damp soil in temperate and tropical climes, where they feed on decaying plant material, fungi, bacteria, excrement and dead insects.

Diplurans have a worldwide distribution, occurring in dark, humid places such as soil or under bark.

Proturans occupy moist leaf litter and soil, commonly to depths of 23cm (9in), and feed on fungus and decaying plant matter.

Bristletails and silverfish are found in varied environments throughout the world. They feed on algae, lichen and plant debris.

Bristletails (Archaeognatha)

With elongated cylindrical bodies up to 20mm (0.79in) long, bristletails are shaped rather like a turnip. They have

Below: Silverfish have a silver body and scuttle across damp surfaces.

long antennae, six legs and two long cerci with a long central filament, giving them the appearance of having three bristles for tails.

These insects comprise about 350 species in two families, Meinertellidae and Machilidae. Bristletails can be

either nocturnal or diurnal. Little is known of their breeding habits. On hatching, the young look like miniature versions of the adults.

Silverfish (Thysanura)

They are 2–22mm (0.08–0.87in) long, with flat elongate shiny silver bodies. Their antennae are long and they have two cerci and a tail-like telson at their rear.

There are 370 species in four families: Lepidotrichidae, Nicoletiidae, Lepismatidae and Maindroniidae.

Most species are nocturnal omnivores, scavenging under bark, in leaf litter. Males secrete silk that they suspend sperm droplets on for the female to take up. The eggs hatch into nymphs that, apart from size, are the same as the adults in appearance.

Like bristletails, silverfish can run fast, but unlike them they do not jump.

MAYFLIES AND STONEFLIES

The mayflies belong to the order Ephemeroptera and have been present since the Carboniferous.
Stoneflies are in the order Plecoptera, present since the Permian. Both are found near water and have
aquatic nymphs that are important components of the food chain, especially for fish.

Mayflies (Ephemeroptera)

The word Ephemeroptera is derived from the Greek 'ephemera' (fleeting), and 'pteron' (wing) – they are short-lived winged insects. They are small to medium-sized, soft-bodied insects with two pairs of wings: two forewings and two smaller hindwings, all of which are closed vertically above the body. They have short antennae, large compound eyes and three ocelli (light sensors), and at the rear end have two long cerci and a long 'tail' filament.

Their common names include shadfly, day fly, Canadian 'soldier fly' and fishfly. The adults do not feed, but the larvae feed on diatoms, algae and detritus, or are carnivorous.

The order is split into two suborders, the Schistonota (split-backs) and the Pannota (fused-backs) with approximately 2,500 species in 23 families. The two suborders can be distinguished by looking at the nymphs; the Schistonota nymphs have wing pads (immature wings) that are separate on each side of their thorax (next section after head), while the Pannota nymphs have their wing pads stuck together on their thorax (back). For adults identification is by the differing wing venation (lines on wing surface) of species.

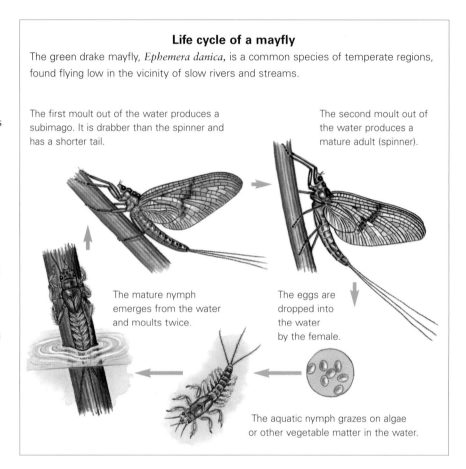

Life cycle of a mayfly

The green drake mayfly, *Ephemera danica*, is a common species of temperate regions, found flying low in the vicinity of slow rivers and streams.

The first moult out of the water produces a subimago. It is drabber than the spinner and has a shorter tail.

The second moult out of the water produces a mature adult (spinner).

The mature nymph emerges from the water and moults twice.

The eggs are dropped into the water by the female.

The aquatic nymph grazes on algae or other vegetable matter in the water.

Left: The dun is the newly emerged winged form of the mayfly; the spinner is the adult form following the second out-of-water moult. The spent are dead or dying mayflies, often seen on the water surface. Emergence of adult mayflies is usually from May to August depending on species.

The nymphs in the families have different feeding habits. Some are carnivorous, or eat decaying matter or a mixture of the two. Others are herbivores that feed on decaying plant matter.

The newly emerged adults swarm above the water surface seeking out a potential mate. The male's long front legs hold on to their chosen female and mating takes place in the air. The female then, depending on species, drops eggs singly or in batches into the water, or places them purposefully on submerged vegetation. The adult lives for approximately one day to one week, and dies soon after mating.

The young that hatch, though, can live up to three years and are known as nymphs, but they do not resemble the adult form. Instead, they are wingless and have chewing mouth-parts. Breathing is by external gills along the sides of the body and in certain species there are three feathery tails as well. Insects have a tracheal system for allowing oxygenated air to passively reach their body tissues via a series of holes along their abdomens, but in these nymphs the system is sealed. The nymphs will undergo as many as 50 moults before maturing.

When a nymph has reached maturity and emerges from the water, it moults twice before it is fully adult. The first moult out of water produces a subadult that can fly, but the second moult produces the fully active adult.

Stoneflies (Plecoptera)

The name of the stonefly order Plecoptera is derived from Greek; 'plectos' (pleated) and 'pteron' (wing). They range in body size from 3–48mm (0.12–1.89in) with a maximum membranous wingspan of 10cm (4in). Their bodies are soft, dark brown or black, and slender, and they have bulging eyes, three ocelli and long antennae. The front wings are long and narrow compared to the hindwings, which are pleated when closed and lie flat against the body. The rear end has two long cerci.

Freshwater fishermen model artificial stoneflies (nymph or adult form) that are also referred to as salmon fly, trout fly or willow fly as lures for trout. All stages/ages of nymphal instars are present year-round in water bodies and are prey items for fish. When depositing their eggs the females disturb the water surface, attracting the predatory fish.

There are 2,000 species in 15 families divided between two suborders. They have worldwide distribution mainly in temperate cool regions.

The eggs when deposited undergo diapause (rest) from two weeks to two months (dependent on species) and when water temperature and the day length are suitable, will hatch.

The adults are recognized by their flattened bodies and their wings, which in most species extend beyond the end of their body. As adults they are nocturnal and by day seek out dark places to hide, such as under stones or bark. Nymphs with an omnivorous diet will not feed on emerging as adults, but the herbivorous nymphs tend to produce adults that do feed.

Males attract a mate by drumming or tapping on a terrestrial surface – single taps or more complex 'songs' that in turn are replied to by a female, and the two search each other out. The slimy egg mass, of up to 1,000 eggs, is deposited and adheres to plant or rock

Habitats of mayflies and stoneflies

Mayfly nymphs live in an aquatic habitat, which may be fast/slow running rivers, ditches, ponds, streams or lakes. Some species breed in water bodies with a gravelly bottom, while others prefer a silt or muddy substrate.

These insects have a worldwide distribution, but are found particularly in temperate regions where they require clean unpolluted and well-oxygenated water to complete their life cycle.

Stoneflies like well-oxygenated, pollution-free, flowing water in habitats such as streams and rivers with a rocky bottom. Lakes, sandy areas and damp areas also support certain species but less is known about these. These insects are well adapted to cold water conditions and, as such, a higher diversity of species are found in temperate zones, where they are mostly nocturnal.

surfaces or lodges in crevices within the water column. On hatching, the nymphs have the appearance of an earwig with two tails. The nymphs undergo up to 30 moults over one to four years, before finally emerging from the water as adults. They are eagerly eaten by many birds.

Below: A stonefly nymph lies on the bottom of a river, clinging tightly in the current.

Stonefly nymphs have an array of defence mechanisms to prevent being eaten, such as feigning death, reflex bleeding and using known 'boltholes' within their area of foraging, such as under pebbles and rocks.

Below: Stoneflies emerge and moult at the edges of watercourses, usually when dark, leaving behind their shed skin or 'shuck'. They survive for around three to four weeks before dying.

DRAGONFLIES AND DAMSELFLIES

The order Odonata is divided into two suborders – the dragonflies (Anisoptera) and the damselflies (Zygoptera). A third suborder, the Anisozygoptera, is sometimes recognized, but these are mainly extinct forms. Odonata is derived from the Greek 'odontos' (toothed), referring to the mandibles.

Dragonflies (Anisoptera)

The suborder name Anisoptera means 'unequal wings', which refers to the broader hindwings compared to the forewings. There are five families, with 3,000 living species, told apart by their adult colours and their body shapes.

Dragonflies are large, colourful, long-bodied insects with amazing flying abilities. Their two pairs of wings are independent and capable of changing their angle, wing beat frequency and depth of wing beat, allowing dragonflies to fly backward, if necessary. Their thorax is packed with flight muscles and at rest the wings lie straight out sideways.

Dragonflies have large heads and compound eyes that have near 360-degree stereoscopic vision. A dragonfly's eye has 30,000 lenses (compared to a human's single lens) and they have been seen to home in on prey up to 12m (40ft) away. They also have strong biting mouthparts and paired claspers at their rear end. Their legs are used for standing or grabbing prey on the wing, but they are unable to walk well on them. All dragonflies are predators using their excellent sight to hunt prey.

Outside the polar regions they are found worldwide but more than half live in the tropics.

Dragonflies are active by day, and hunt other flying insects in the air. The pairing and position of the male and female during mating is known

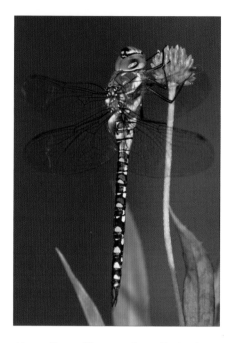

Above: Dragonflies are robust. Their wings are held open when they are at rest.

as the 'copulation wheel'. This describes the coupling, where the male grasps the female behind her head with claspers while she raises her abdomen under herself and forward. Mating can occur while perched or in flight. The eggs are laid either directly into water, attached to weeds, or in marginal plants. The female uses her ovipositor to cut a slit in the vegetation and then lay her eggs within it.

On hatching, the nymphs are active hunters of tadpoles, fish fry and other

Below: Dragonfly nymphs are voracious hunters, capable of killing small fish.

Life cycle of a a dragonfly

The emperor dragonfly, *Anax imperator*. This widespread species is also one of the largest. It is found over much of Europe and Asia, and also in North Africa.

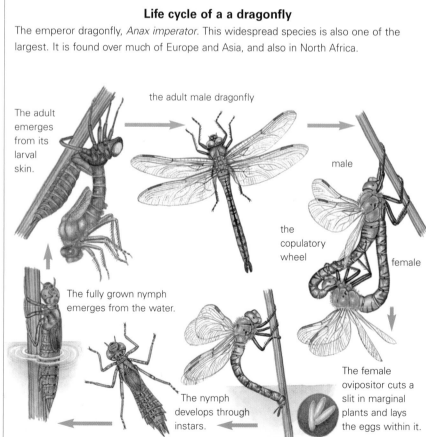

The adult emerges from its larval skin.

the adult male dragonfly

male

the copulatory wheel

female

The fully grown nymph emerges from the water.

The nymph develops through instars.

The female ovipositor cuts a slit in marginal plants and lays the eggs within it.

small creatures, including their own kind. They capture their prey with an elongated, hinged lower lip (labium) that shoots forward, grabbing the victim with clawed paired palps located on the end. This feature is known as the 'mask'. At rest the mask is held folded underneath the head and thorax, sometimes extending back beyond the front legs. The dragonfly nymph expands and contracts its abdomen to move water over its gills within the abdomen, and can squeeze the water out rapidly for a short burst of underwater jet propulsion.

The nymphs undergo between ten and 20 moults, and live from three months up to ten years. When mature, the nymph emerges from the water on to vegetation where it perches and moults into the winged adult form.

Damselflies (Zygoptera)

Zygoptera means 'equal-sized wings'. The hindwings are similar in shape to the front wings.

Damselflies are weaker fliers than dragonflies, with colourful but delicate and much smaller bodies. They have large heads, strong biting mouthparts and widely separated compound eyes, with more than 80 per cent of the brain devoted to visual processing – the same as dragonflies. They have paired claspers at their rear end and their legs are used for standing or grabbing prey on the wing, but they are unable to walk well on them. Damselflies are all carnivorous insects, using their excellent sight to hunt prey.

Damselflies have two pairs of elongated membranous wings with a strong cross vein and many small veins that criss-cross, as well as a small coloured patch, adding strength and flexibility. Damselflies can close their wings over their body at rest due to a hinge, whereas dragonflies cannot. They are not as restricted to sunny days as dragonflies, with males often defending their territories even when it is overcast.

All damselfly females possess an ovipositor. They are all predators, including the nymphs, which hunt by stalking in submerged vegetation.

Habitats of dragonflies and damselflies

Dragonflies are commonly found near fresh water but are in no way restricted to it; as strong fliers (50kmh/30mph) they can travel many miles to forage and some species even migrate over the sea.

Damselflies tend to be rather fluttery in flight. They are found around water and breed in varying freshwater flows, from still and stagnant to fast-moving, depending on the species.

When mating, damselflies form a 'copulatory wheel' like dragonflies. Mating may take from a few minutes to several hours, and when laying eggs, they may stay in the tandem position, the male guarding his mate. The eggs of damselflies are cylindrical, whereas dragonfly eggs are ovoid in shape. The places and manner in which they lay their eggs are similar to dragonflies. In the tropics, development of the nymph may be complete in 60 days, whereas in colder temperate climes it may take up to ten years. Development of damselfly nymphs, though, tends to be quicker than dragonflies, with fewer moults necessary, and usually takes approximately one year. Depending on the species, they may breed any number of times in a year, but this is dependent on food availability and water temperature. The eggs may enter a resting stage until the water temperature rises. Adults may live from weeks to a few months. Damselfly nymphs seize prey in the same way as dragonflies, with the elongate extensible, hinged labium or

'mask'. In the damselfly nymph the abdomen is longer and narrower with three fin-like gills projecting from the end, whereas the shorter, stockier dragonfly nymph has gills located inside the abdomen on plates.

Below: Damselflies are very slender and hold their wings closed over their bodies.

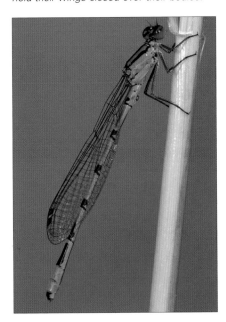

COCKROACHES AND TERMITES, MANTIDS AND EARWIGS

The four orders on these pages contain a wide range of insects. Cockroaches and termites feed mainly on plant matter. Most earwigs are omnivores, while mantids are strictly carnivorous, waiting patiently among the foliage that they mimic for their prey.

Cockroaches (Blattodea)

This order contains cockroaches, of which only one per cent of the 4,000 species are pests to man, the vast majority being harmless. The one per cent that are associated with man are attracted to food and dirty living conditions, and may carry germs on their feet or excrete dangerous viruses and protozoans. Of the other 99 per cent of harmless cockroaches, many are kept as pets, such as the Madagascan hissing cockroach *Gromphadorhina portentosa*, which when threatened expels air from the spiracles (breathing holes on body sides) to produce its characteristic hissing sound.

Cockroaches have flattened, oval-shaped, leathery bodies, with long thin antennae and strong spiny legs suitable for running. The forewings are toughened, protecting the membranous hind pair, and at rest the wings lie flat across the body, overlapping. Cockroaches have chewing and biting mouthparts and they are also able to lap up liquid food. They have large compound eyes and a large flattened plate attached to the thorax that covers part of the head.

Most female cockroaches produce a sex pheromone to attract a mate, and the males often produce 'aphrodisiac' secretions to prepare the female for mating. Courtship can vary from slight

body movements to production of sounds, or even head butting in the Madagascan hissing cockroach. The sperm is transferred in a spermato-phore and the female either lays her eggs in an egg case and buries them, or carries them under her abdomen.

Termites (Isoptera)

Sometimes called 'white ants' due to their coloration, termites are social insects that live in colonies, with reproductives, workers and soldiers of both sexes. They have soft bodies, biting mouthparts, short cerci and simple antennae with 9–30 segments. Termites are mainly tropical or subtropical insects that feed on wood, fresh leaves, leaf litter or soil. They are grouped, according to their feeding or habitat preferences, as subterranean, soil-feeding, dry-wood, damp-wood or grass-eating. Dry-wood termites include some that are pest species of buildings.

Left: The Madagascan hissing cockroach plays an important role as a decomposer in the forests where it lives, helping to break down fallen fruits and other plant matter.

Above: Mantids are also known as praying mantises. This common name derives from the 'praying' pose they adopt when waiting for prey.

To maintain and guard their nests, termites have evolved a reproductive strategy that provides both a workforce and soldiers. The workers are sterile and make up most of the colony, carrying out nest building and repair duties, foraging, taking care of eggs and nymphs and caring for the queen. In lower termites, there may not be a distinct caste system, and nymphs often undertake these duties.

The 'primary reproductives' possess two pairs of wings, and will become the founders of a new colony. After the 'nuptial' flight, they shed their wings and mate, thus becoming king and queen. A colony can take up to two years to establish. The queen termite can grow to 90mm (3.54in), and in some species can produce an egg every three seconds.

In Amazonian forests the total biomass of termites can be ten per cent of the soil fauna and 80 per cent of the fauna of dead wood.

Above: Earwigs like confined, dark spaces.

Above: Termites are among the most common insects on Earth, with a global population measured in the trillions.

Mantids (Mantodea)

Found mainly in warm regions of the world, mantids are elongate, medium to large sized insects, growing up to 25cm (10in) in some South American species. Many are winged, with two leathery forewings and two hindwings. The head is triangular with large forward-facing compound eyes that have binocular vision. The two front legs are adapted to catch prey. Mantids are predators, feeding mainly on insects and spiders. There are about 2,000 species.

The male is generally smaller than the female, and in some species may be eaten by the female after or during mating. The female may lay 6–22 ootheca (egg cases), with 30–300 eggs in each, through her lifetime. The female will attach the ootheca to twigs or stones, and in some species will guard the eggs and even the nymphs for a few days after hatching.

Most mantids fly at night, when they may be preyed on by bats. Bats use ultrasonic clicks to locate prey, and mantids have an ultrasonic detecting 'ear' between their front legs. When harmful frequencies emitted by bats are detected, the mantid takes immediate evasive action, entering into a 'nosedive' if the bat is very close.

Earwigs (Dermaptera)

Earwigs have leathery short forewings and hindwings which are large and membranous, though they rarely fly. They are common, slender, brown or black, elongate 4–80mm (0.16–3.15in) and slightly flattened insects with biting mouthparts and two forceps-like cerci at their rear end, which are their most distinguishing feature. The cerci are curved in males and straight in females. There are about 1,900 species of earwig. Most earwigs are nocturnal and omnivorous, feeding on dead plant material and slow-moving invertebrates. Female earwigs show maternal care.

In temperate climates spring triggers females into constructing a brood chamber under a stone, in a burrow or within rotting vegetation. Mating is performed rear end to rear end, usually with each holding the other's pincers, and at night. The female tends the eggs, turning and cleaning them until they hatch, when she will leave to forage for food. The nymphs pass through four or five instars, but after the first two they disperse, to avoid the risk of the female eating them.

Some earwigs have defensive glands on their abdomens, which produce a noxious liquid that in some can be squirted 10cm (4in).

Most are considered beneficial insects since they eat pest species.

Habitats of mantids, earwigs and termites

Mantids live among tree foliage, flowers or grasses where they are expert ambush predators. They are often the same colour as their surroundings, and many have body outgrowths mimicking flower petals, leaves or twigs to help disguise them.

Most earwigs are free-living but some are parasitic or semi-parasitic on bats or rodents. Earwigs prefer confined humid habitats. They are found worldwide, except in the polar regions, and are most common in tropical areas.

Termites build nests, in fallen wood or above or below ground, in order to shelter the colony. Termite mounds are constructed from soil excavated in the course of digging underground tunnels, or from soil and sand collected on the surface, mixed with saliva and faeces. The interior has an intricate network of tunnels and galleries for movement, and in some species, for the cultivation of fungi. To maintain airflow and an even temperature, vents lead off from some tunnels.

GRASSHOPPERS, LOCUSTS AND CRICKETS

These insects belong to the order Orthoptera, which contains 22,000 species and includes some of the world's most familiar insects. The order name is derived from the Greek words 'orthos' (straight) and 'pteron' (wing). The order has a worldwide distribution with a high diversity in the tropics.

Grasshoppers (Caelifera)

This suborder consists of about 34 families of locusts, grasshoppers, pygmy locusts, bush-hoppers and bush locusts. Caeliferous insects have fewer than 30 segments in their antennae (termed short-horned), a reduced ovipositor and a hearing organ (if present) sited in the abdominal area. The production of sound is usually from the hind legs rubbing against the wings, or in some species, the clicking of the wings in flight.

Body size ranges from 5–11.5cm (2–4.5in) with wingspans up to 22cm (8.5in) and they possess compound eyes. The majority are plant eaters, but a few are omnivorous. Crickets and grasshoppers have stout bodies with large blunt heads and large rear legs adapted for jumping. Wings if present are two tough leathery forewings and a pair of membranous hindwings.

They have relatively short antennae and their chirpy song fills the air in warmer months. Most members of this family are grassland species but some are found in marshy areas. Sound production is either from pegs on the inner hind legs which are rubbed against a hardened vein on the forewing, or the other way around with the pegs on the forewing.

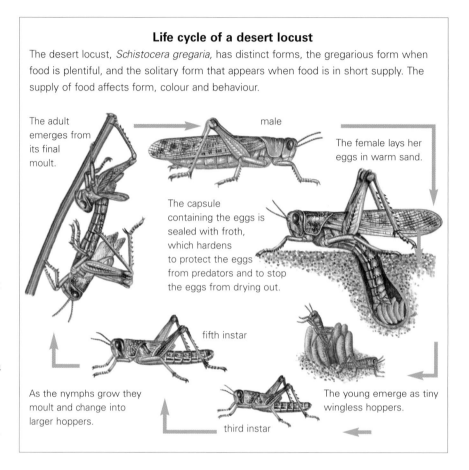

Life cycle of a desert locust

The desert locust, *Schistocera gregaria*, has distinct forms, the gregarious form when food is plentiful, and the solitary form that appears when food is in short supply. The supply of food affects form, colour and behaviour.

The adult emerges from its final moult.

male

The female lays her eggs in warm sand.

The capsule containing the eggs is sealed with froth, which hardens to protect the eggs from predators and to stop the eggs from drying out.

fifth instar

The young emerge as tiny wingless hoppers.

As the nymphs grow they moult and change into larger hoppers.

third instar

The members of the family Tetrigidae include the pygmy locusts, groundhoppers and pygmy grasshoppers. There are approximately 1,400 species. In Australia, a small family, the Cylindrachetidae, known as sandgropers, are an important economic pest. The females remain wingless as adults and resemble larvae, with a very elongated, cylindrical body, up to 70mm (2.76in) long, short, flattened front legs held beside the head, and simple eyes, all of which are adaptations for burrowing. Two species are also found in New Guinea and Argentina.

These are all predominantly tropical species, with many still undescribed.

The males sing to attract a mate. When mating occurs the male deposits a sperm package into the female's

Left: Grasshoppers have long bodies and many have large wings. Most are well camouflaged but a few are surprisingly colourful.

Habitats of crickets, locusts and grasshoppers

Few grass-dominated habitats are without crickets, grasshoppers or locusts, and grass and other plant matter makes up a large part of their diet. Most are rather secretive and may be heard rather than seen.

In the tropics, species are also found in the tree canopy or living among lichens and mosses, but the main families are well represented around the world in all habitats that support plants. These include deserts, bogs, marshes, grassland and woodland. Generally, they are ground-dwelling insects that feed mainly on grass during the day, but many grasshoppers can fly well. Locusts in particular are known for their long migrations in search of food.

ovipositor, and when the eggs have been fertilized she deposits them 20–50mm (0.8–2in) underground. In temperate regions, the eggs overwinter and can stay up to nine months underground until conditions are warm enough for hatching. They hatch into worm-like creatures, but on reaching the surface they discard this outer coating to reveal a nymph that will then undergo four to six nymphal instars. Life expectancy of an adult is around three months – they die in autumn with the next generation remaining as eggs underground.

Locusts change colour and behaviour at high population densities. Locusts are an important economic pest species capable, in their enormous swarms, of destroying vast areas of vegetation and crops, in places such as Africa, South America and the Middle East. The species *Schistocerca gregaria* is a significant pest, able to fly great distances in huge swarms, producing between two and five generations in a year and seriously affecting harvests and often devastating crops.

Crickets (Ensifera)

Ensifera is Latin for 'sword-bearer' and refers to the shape of the ovipositor. Crickets are distinguished from grasshoppers by their long antennae (over 30 segments) and ovipositor, and the fact that they have their hearing organ on their front legs. Some females

Below: Crickets are most easily identified by their long antennae. Unlike grasshoppers they tend to walk rather than fly or hop.

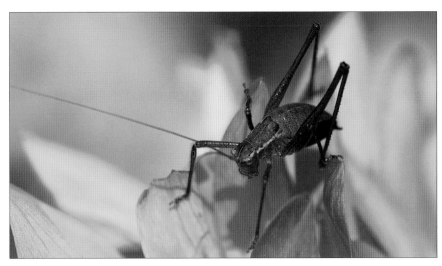

show maternal care. They are mainly nocturnal insects with a lifespan of over one year. Many crickets make loud rasping and repetitive calls to attract a mate.

Within the suborder are between four and six superfamilies (depending on classification used) and 12 families. The family Tettigoniidae are commonly known in the USA as katydids and elsewhere as bush crickets (or confusingly as long-horned grasshoppers). There are 5,000 species that are herbivorous, saprophagous or predacious, with some pest species. Their antennae can be as long as their body and most inhabit plant foliage. The majority of species are found in the tropics and they sing by rubbing their forewings together; the left wing, having the pegs, is rubbed over the right wing. Gryllidae is the family of 'true crickets'. It has approximately 1,500 species with moderately flattened bodies and long antennae. They are mostly nocturnal. Sound is produced in this family by the forewings where the right wing is toothed and is drawn across the left wing.

The Gryllotalpidae family are more commonly known as 'mole crickets'. They are capable of clumsy flying – males manage up to 8km (5 miles) in the mating season – and are thick-bodied with enormous shovel-like front legs for digging. They excavate tunnels in the soil to feed on plant roots and invertebrates, and to live in; males adapt a tunnel with a bell chamber to amplify their song.

STICK AND LEAF INSECTS

The order Phasmatodea contains the stick and leaf insects, strange creatures often kept as pets. They resemble grasshoppers and crickets in some respects but are adapted for camouflage with often bizarre body shapes. The name of the order is derived from the Greek 'phasma' meaning spectre or apparition.

Division of the order

There are three families in the order: Phylliidae, Phasmatidae and Timematidae. The Phylliidae contains the 'true' leaf insects which are found from South and South-east Asia to Australia. The Phasmatidae contain the vast majority of stick insects, while the Timematidae contains just a single genus of stick insect which has three segments in the tarsi (the end section of the leg) rather than five.

The key defining feature of their order is that all members are superb at camouflage and mimicking their habitat. Through the course of evolution they have adopted the appearance of twigs, twigs with lichens, mosses, and even bird faeces. Some of the leaf insects are remarkably similar to the plants they live among.

Stick insects (Phasmatidae and Timematidae)

Sometimes known as ghost sticks or walking sticks, stick insects are elongate 10–30cm (4–12in), slender and cylindrical with a variable body shape. They have long legs, short, leathery forewings and large membranous hindwings (in some species the wings are absent), thread-like antennae, small compound eyes and biting mouthparts.

Leaf insects (Phylliidae)

Leaf insects tend to be broad, flat and leaf-shaped. The leaf insects are impressive at mimicking leaves, often including the appearance of mildew, insect feeding damage and leaf veins. When seen they are hard to mistake for any other insect.

Above: This stick insect mimics the colours of its background, which effectively camouflage it from predators.

Common features

In many species males are rare or absent and the females produce viable eggs without fertilization (a process known as parthenogenesis). Males, if required for sexual reproduction, are generally smaller than females. They may be attracted by pheromones. In some, such as the North American species, *Diapheromera veliei*, the males compete by kicking out legs with spines at one another in an attempt to win a female.

The unmated female lays eggs that have just her genetic material, to produce female clones (which are genetically identical to her). The eggs resemble plant seeds, and depending on phasmid species the female may just drop them from where she is and lightly cover them in sand or soil, or stick them to foliage. Some species have eggs with an extra bit on the top which juts out to attract ants. When ants collect these from the ground and return to the nest, they eat the nutrient-rich top, leaving the egg untouched. This adaptation gives ants a rich food parcel and the phasmid egg a safe environment in which to develop. The egg, depending on the

---

Life cycle of a stick insect

The male of the species has stronger wings and it is he who flies to find a mate. Stick and leaf insects lay eggs that can take weeks or months to hatch depending on species. The eggs may be carried by ants far from the point where they were deposited.

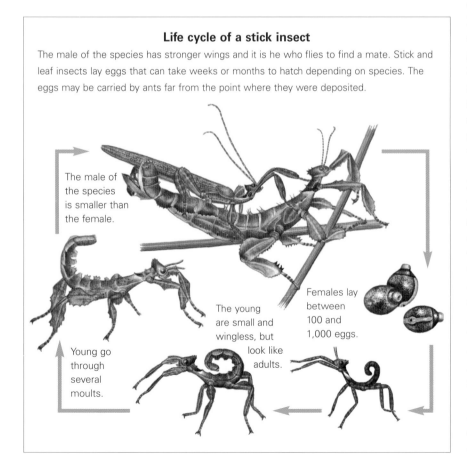

The male of the species is smaller than the female.

The young are small and wingless, but look like adults.

Females lay between 100 and 1,000 eggs.

Young go through several moults.

species, takes from one month to a year to develop and hatch. The hatched nymphs look like miniature adults and go through between two and eight moults before maturity.

Phasmids have the ability to feign death when disturbed, falling to the ground and remaining motionless until the danger has passed. Another strategy is to willingly shed a limb in an effort to escape. Although this may seem extreme to us, by losing a limb they are able to save their life. Many winged species flash open brightly coloured wings, or rustle them to startle predators, while others simply fly away and are lost in the vegetation. The nymphs of some species (*Extatosoma tiaratum*) are thought to mimic ants to prevent attack. Other species, such as *Eurycnema* from Australia, use spines on their spiky legs to strike out. *Anisomorpha buprestoides* from the south-east USA has warning colours on its body, and dispenses a foul-smelling liquid from glands on the upper part of its thorax and around its mouthparts. Stick insects are popular as pets and many species may be kept in a vivarium. Most will eat a range of food plants and will reproduce readily, producing many tiny young.

Below: This phasmid has flanges along its abdomen that resemble a leaf.

Habitats of stick and leaf insects

These are all herbivorous slow-moving insects, living and feeding within foliage and distributed mainly in tropical and subtropical regions. They are found in a variety of habitats including wet and dry forests and grassland. During the day, they tend to hide on the forest floor, under leaves or among twigs where they have adapted to sway gently like the surrounding foliage in a breeze, but at night, they come out to feed.

Some species have the ability to change colour to match their surroundings. Some are like twigs, many even with sharp spines, while others are flattened and flanged, like leaves.

Below: The variety of shapes among phasmids surprises many people. The intricate patterns on the body of this species help to give it camouflage.

Below: Leaf insects mimic the foliage of the plants on which they feed. This disguise works as effective camouflage from predators.

BOOKLICE, BARK-LICE, WEB SPINNERS, ZORAPTERANS, THRIPS AND PARASITIC LICE

The orders described on these pages all contain tiny insects. Some are so small that they may live on our bodies or share our homes in significant numbers without us ever noticing them. Others are irritating parasites of other animals, including humans.

Booklice and bark-lice (Psocoptera)

This order includes booklice and bark lice, which are active, fast-running, small 1–10mm (0.04–0.39in), soft-bodied insects whose coloration matches their surroundings. They have protruding compound eyes, thin antennae and simple, chewing mouth-parts. The wings, if present (booklice are wingless), are two fore and two hind, with the forewings slightly larger.

There are about 3,000 species distributed worldwide. These insects feed on plant material, algae, lichens or fungi.

A limited number of species reproduce by parthenogenesis. The eggs are laid singly or in groups covered with silk. They may be left exposed or placed under bark or vegetation. The nymphs usually pass through six instars, and stay in nymphal groups until adulthood.

Web spinners (Embioptera)

The common name of these insects comes from their ability to spin silk galleries from threads exuded from a gland in the front leg. They are small-to medium-sized elongate, brown insects with kidney-shaped eyes, biting mouthparts and short legs. The front

Life cycle of a booklouse

The booklouse, *Ectopsocus briggsi*, is a common species found on bark and also on books and paper. Booklice live for up to six months. They lay eggs that hatch after 11 days. The eggs become mature adults within 15 days, so infestations can occur quickly.

the female

The wings develop as the nymph matures.

The female lays oblong eggs in clumps on leaves or bark.

The appearance of the insect in the nymphal stages (right and below) is similar to the adult.

legs have a swollen area where the silk gland is located. Males possess two pairs of hind and forewings, but the females are wingless.

There are between eight and ten families (depending on the system of classification used) with 170 species.

The female lays her eggs within the gallery and covers them with silk. She remains guarding them in the egg stage and in some species will even feed the first instars with pre-chewed food. Web spinners look rather like miniature earwigs, to which they may be related.

Left: A bird-louse grips the feathers of a peacock. Almost all birds and fowl are affected by some kind of lice.

Zorapterans (Zoraptera)

A number of this order are tiny termite-like, delicate, white to brown coloured insects. The dominant forms are blind and wingless, but they can produce winged, eyed offspring that can disperse to new areas.

There is a single family containing 30 species, mostly from tropical regions with four species known in warm temperate regions.

Zorapterans feed on fungi and predate and scavenge nematodes, mites and other small invertebrates in damp bark or logs.

Males offer 'gifts' of secretions from a gland on their heads to induce females to mate with them. Pairs mate two or three times to produce eggs.

Thrips (Thysanoptera)

This order contains the thrips. They are small 0.5–12mm (0.02–0.47in) yellow-brown or black-bodied, winged insects. There are approximately 5,000 species worldwide.

Thrips have only one mandible in their mouthparts, no cerci, and their wings have fringes of hair along the edges. The eyes are compound and their bodies are slender.

In some species, males fight for the right to mate, sometimes to the death, and mating occurs as the females lay their egg mass. The development of the offspring involves three nymphal stages and two pupal stages before adulthood and sexual maturity.

Parasitic lice (Phthiraptera)

There are approximately 3,150 species of lice distributed worldwide. Parasitic lice feed on the skin debris, secretions or blood of larger hosts, mainly birds and mammals, including humans.

Parasitic lice are small to minute 1–10mm (0.04–0.39in) insects with flattened bodies, and their mouthparts are either chewing mandibles or sucking stylets. Eyes are small or absent, antennae are short and stout with between three and five segments. Their body surface has many sensory hairs, heads are broad in biting lice and conical in sucking lice, and their legs are short with claws for gripping the feathers or hairs of their hosts. Many lice are host-specific, either to a group of similar birds or mammals, or to one single species.

The sucking lice suborder Anoplura feed on rodents. Two species feed on humans: *Phthirus pubis*, the pubic louse which is broad, squat, and moves little, and *Pediculus humanus*, which moves by its short front legs. It has two subspecies, one of which is the head louse and the other is the body louse, which lives on or in clothes and on body hair.

Above: Thrips are often found on flowers, sometimes in large numbers. They feed by piercing and sucking the plant tissues.

A female louse typically lays up to 100 eggs, which are fastened to hair or feathers with fast-acting waterproof glue. The nymphs undergo three nymphal stages which may last from two weeks to three months depending on species. The lice then continue the rest of their lives on that host. If removed from the host the louse will die within a few days. The human body louse attaches her eggs to clothing, especially at the seams. The adults will use the clothing as a hiding place between feeds. Lice can cause skin complaints and severe irritation and sores if persistent or present in numbers. Head lice in particular are a recurring problem in children, especially where many children meet, as at school. Human lice can also spread microbes such as that which causes typhoid fever.

There are also two suborders of chewing lice. More than 2,500 species parasitize birds or mammals feeding on skin, feathers, secretions or blood, some causing irritation.

The order Rhynchophthirina consists of only two species, which feed exclusively on either elephants or warthogs. They have specialized biting mouthparts on the end of a snout, which are used to bore through the host's tough skin. Other chewing lice attack sheep, dogs and various species of bird.

Habitats of booklice, bark-lice, web spinners, zorapterans, thrips and parasitic lice

Most thrips are found on plants where they feed on sap by making a hole with their mandibles then sucking the juices out with other mouthparts. A large number also feed on pollen and are useful flower pollinators. Some species live in leaf litter where they feed on fungal spores, and other species are predacious on other insects such as mites. Some thrips live in colonies with soldiers that protect other individuals.

Web spinners live in small communities. The silken tunnels are expanded to find new food sources as the need arises. Only females and nymphs feed, mainly on lichens, litter, mosses and dead plant material.

Booklice and bark-lice form gregarious groups under bark, leaf litter or wood dust. They are considered beneficial to the trees on which they live. Zorapterans live under bark or in rotting wood.

BUGS

Hemiptera is the largest order of insects with incomplete metamorphosis. There are estimated to be 82,000 species of bug worldwide, comprising about eight to ten per cent of all known insect species. The order includes pond skaters, cicadas, leaf-hoppers, aphids, scale insects and whiteflies.

Common features

The term 'bug' is often used for all insects, but should strictly apply only to the Hemiptera. All Hemiptera possess specialized mouthparts modified into a proboscis, which can appear like a beak. It typically forms a slender, piercing tube used for stabbing the host, either plant or animal, and sucking liquids. In herbivorous bugs the saliva injected into the host's tissue generally causes local necrosis in plants, whereas in predatory species, the saliva is highly toxic and can paralyse relatively large prey.

The majority of bugs are also characterized by the structure of their wings, which are hardened near the base but membranous at the ends, hence their order's name, which literally means half wing in Greek ('hemysis' – half; 'pteron' – wing).

Hemipterans have special organs which enable them to produce sounds. Some (for example cicadas) produce sounds by vibration of a pair of parchment-like tymbals in the base of the abdomen. In other families,

Below: Pond skaters are predatory bugs which hunt on the surface of freshwater habitats, catching other creatures which tumble in.

Above: Leaf-hoppers have piercing mouthparts and feed on plant sap.

sound is produced by different mechanisms, such as rubbing the wings over a striate area at the base of the abdomen. Some species are also well known for the secretion of aromatic compounds as a defence against predators.

Bugs range from minute, wingless scales to the fish-eating giant water bug (*Lethocerus maximus*) which can attain a length of 11.6cm (4.5in). Large bugs are more slender and thus less heavy than most other insects of a similar length, such as the beetles.

Many bug species are significant pests of crops and gardens. Among the worst are the many species of aphids, scale-insects and whiteflies. Injection of

saliva may be an important factor in the transmission of micro-organisms, especially plant viruses, which make these bugs serious vectors of plant diseases. Blood-feeding species, on the other hand, often carry potentially deadly infections. Some species, however, have a positive use, such as the scale insects, which are used in the production of dyes.

In general, hemipterans have simple or incomplete metamorphosis, in which the young, called nymphs, are similar to adults in shape. The wings develop and increase in size at each moult and become functional after the last moult, as do the reproductive organs. Many species among the aphids can lay unfertilized eggs that are genetically identical to their mother, a reproductive strategy called parthenogenesis. There can be one to several generations per year. Most bugs produce eggs which are laid inside plant tissue or on plants, or other substrates.

The following suborders, each containing species which share morphological and/or ecological similarities, are often recognized.

Below: Stink bugs, or shield bugs, produce foul-smelling liquid to aid their defence.

Stink bugs, bed bugs, leaf bugs and water bugs (Heteroptera)

This is the largest of the suborders and contains many familiar bugs. There are approximately 50,000 species, commonly called 'true bugs'. It includes well-known species such as water striders, pond skaters, water and marine bugs, bed bugs and stink bugs.

Species of Heteroptera are characterized by having their wings divided into two areas, hence their name, which means 'different wings', one part thickened and opaque and the other part membranous and usually transparent. Some species, such as the water striders, have lost their wings, while others have inefficient wings and are unable to fly.

The group is also characterized by the variety of form and colours displayed by the different species. These are often used as a defence mechanism. Some have adopted a camouflage technique in which the insects appear similar to their surroundings, while others mimic features of other organisms. Many species also have bright coloration, often used as a warning for predators. Shield bugs are among the most spectacular of all bugs due to their iridescent or metallic colours.

Nearly all species possess scent glands in the thorax, and stink bugs produce an irritant, smelly defensive secretion when disturbed.

About 60 per cent are diurnal, active plant feeders with well-developed eyes and wings, although many variations and exceptions exist.

Left: A bed bug feeds on human skin.

Habitats of bugs

Although less well known than beetles or butterflies, bugs are a diverse group of insects which very often live in association with humans and occur in a wide variety of habitats. Several species, such as the water boatmen and water scorpions, are aquatic.

The well-known pond skaters or water striders are also associated with water but only use the water surface. Another group is truly marine and some have been found on the surface of the ocean hundreds of miles from land. All aquatic species are predatory but the majority of bugs are plant feeders. A minority feed on other insects, while others are external parasites, feeding on the blood of large vertebrates.

They feed on various plants and suck the juices of fruits. Other species are predatory or external parasites.

The typical life cycle of a heteropteran bug consists of the egg, five nymph stages and the adult stage. They usually live in the same habitat as the adult and have identical lifestyles.

Some species are of agricultural importance, feeding on the reproductive parts of the plants such as flowers, ovaries or fruits. Others damage the plants by feeding on stems and roots, for example the chinch bugs *Blissus*, which occasionally wipe out entire lawns. Many species, such as lace bugs, attack and damage ornamental plants.

Moss bugs (Coleorrhyncha)

Forming the suborder Coleorrhyncha, moss bugs are limited to South America, Australia and New Zealand. There are 25 known species, most of which look like plant hoppers. They vary from 2–4mm (0.08–0.16in) in length. They are generally flattened, greenish or brownish with a broad head and lateral extensions. They feed mainly on mosses and usually live in moist habitats such as damp leaf litter on the forest floor; a few species have been found living in caves. Moss bugs are flightless.

Below: Aphids damage plants, slowing their growth by feeding on their sap. They also make a tasty meal for ladybirds.

Jumping plant lice, aphids, whiteflies, scale insects and (Sternorrhyncha)

These common insects are found in many different ecosystems throughout the world. They range in size from 0.1–10cm (0.04–4in) long, and also vary greatly in shape and colour. All species are plant feeders and many are considered as major pests. This group of insects is well known for the cotton-like wax produced by some of the species. The eggs are typically deposited on plant surfaces. Some species jump or fly, but they are predominantly quite sedentary, specialized for rapid feeding and reproduction. Parthenogenesis is widespread and can be alternated with sexual reproduction. Very often the juveniles differ morphologically from adults.

Jumping plant lice

These are found in most regions with the majority in the tropics. They are brightly coloured and range from 1–8mm (0.04–0.31in). Their common name refers to their ability to jump when disturbed. They all feed on woody plants. Many plant pests cause damage in the form of galls or poor plant growth.

Aphids

Also known as greenflies or plant lice, aphids are probably the most universally recognized members of this group, with about 250 species considered as serious pests of crops

and ornamental plants. They are minute insects ranging from 1–10mm (0.04–0.39in) in length. They are distributed throughout the world but are most common in temperate zones. Aphids typically travel short distances by walking or by being transported by ants, but they can disperse over great distances if carried by winds.

Many members of this order feed only on one species of plant; others are more opportunistic and feed on hundreds of species.

Aphids and their relatives tend to live in aggregations on their host plants. Many species form specialized relationships with ants, which are attracted to their excretions of honeydew and in return protect them from predators and move them about their host plants.

Aphids can reproduce asexually as well as sexually. Some lay eggs while others give birth to live young. Typically there are six stages of development: the egg, four nymph stages and the adult stage. Aphids live from 20 to 40 days but they are able to reproduce rapidly and some can produce over 40 generations of offspring. There are about 4,500 aphid species known.

Whiteflies

Adult whiteflies have a wingspan of 4mm (0.16in) or less. Roughly 1,200 species have been described. Whiteflies typically reproduce sexually, with unfertilized eggs becoming males. There are six stages of development: the egg, three nymph stages, the pupa stage and the adult. Many species are considered economically important, as pests of crop plants. They feed on plant tissues, typically on the underside of plant leaves, and all feeding stages produce honeydew. The most recognized pest of this group is the sweet potato whitefly. This pest is thought to carry more than 70 different viruses.

Left: Frog-hoppers, or spittlebugs, surround themselves with froth as nymphs. This is known as cuckoo-spit and can be highly visible on foliage.

Above: Aphids are significant plant pests.

Scale insects

These insects are the most diverse group among the Sternorrhyncha. There are about 8,000 species found worldwide on a wide range of plants. Most of them are plant parasites, feeding on sap, though a few species feed on fungi. They can vary greatly in appearance, from shiny pearl-like insects to insects covered with wax. They vary from 1–5mm (0.04–0.19in) in length. Adult females are not very mobile and mostly stay attached to the plant they have parasitized. They secrete a waxy substance for protection which makes them look like scales,

Below: Scale insects are a major problem for gardeners and commercial growers.

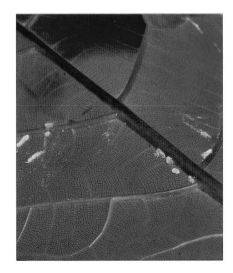

hence the name. Scale insects can be hermaphrodite, reproducing asexually or sexually. Eggs can be laid outside the body, in a protective sac, or withheld in the body, in which case live birth occurs.

Cicadas, frog-hoppers and leaf-hoppers (Auchenorrhyncha)

This is a diverse order, including familiar species such as cicadas as well as many less well-known groups. In this group, the rostrum (beak) arises from under the back of the head.

These species range in size from 0.2–10cm (0.08–4in) with wingspans up to 20cm (8in). There are about 17,000 species described, all terrestrial plant feeders.

Cicadas

About 4,000 species of cicadas are known. They reach lengths of 10cm (4in) although some are only 10mm (0.39in) long. Their most distinctive features are a stout body, large head and large eyes, as well as long and usually transparent wings. They are best known for their loud, high-pitched buzzing songs, produced by the males to attract the females.

Frog-hoppers

Spittlebugs or frog-hoppers are characterized by the frothy masses of 'spittle' produced by the nymphs. About 3,000 species have been described, most of them tropical. Their hind legs are long and adapted for leaping, hence their common name. Most species feed on sap from herbaceous plants or trees, and commonly live in grasslands with the nymphs feeding on roots.

Leaf-hoppers and tree hoppers

Found mainly in tropical America leaf-hoppers and tree hoppers occur in rainforests, savannas and deserts. They are extremely diverse. Many species mimic the substrate they live on in both shape and colour, some resembling thorns with spiny projections, or other plant parts. Many members of this group are gregarious, with young and adults feeding together. They tend to be active during

Life cycle of a bug

The harlequin cabbage bug, *Murgantia histrionica,* can decimate crops by sucking out the sap. Bugs go through incomplete metamorphosis, with the nymphs looking not unlike miniature versions of the adults. Nymphs hatch from the barrel-shaped eggs.

adult

fifth instar

The barrel-shaped eggs are laid in clusters on foliage.

The nymphs lack wings but resemble the adult.

first instar

fourth instar

third instar

second instar

the day. Some nymphs are tended by ants and parental care is also common. They feed on a wide range of host plants, including herbs, grasses, shrubs and trees. The adults are often highly mobile and can migrate long distances, which makes them especially effective as transmitters of plant diseases, especially viruses.

Plant-hoppers

Fulgorids, as plant-hoppers are known, are common in nearly all habitats worldwide. They range from 0.4–10cm (0.16–4in) in length, with wingspans of up to 15cm (6in). Species are diverse and sometimes they have bizarre body forms, with a bulging, disproportionate head. Some species have large colourful eye-spots on their hindwings to startle predators. All species are plant-sap feeders: some feed

on trees or shrubs, others on fungi. Most plant-hoppers spend their entire adult life on foliage, but the majority live underground as nymphs, feeding on grass roots, or in ant nests. Some species are of agricultural significance as pests, because of the plant pathogens they transmit when feeding, or because of the sticky honeydew they excrete. About 10,000 species have been described.

Right: A cicada has left behind its shell in its final moult. Cicadas are more often heard than seen. The sounds they make can travel more than a mile.

CADDIS FLIES, ALDER-FLIES, SNAKE FLIES, LACEWINGS AND SCORPION FLIES

The insects on these pages are a diverse group. All are winged adults and most are quite small, but they include a variety of herbivores, predators and scavengers. The lacewings and relatives are very varied in appearance, and some are quite large.

Caddis flies (Trichoptera)

With about 7,000 different species, caddis flies are easily recognized thanks to their translucent wings, covered with very thin hair.

Larvae are surrounded by a case built out of a variety of materials such as wood, grains of sand, or leaves to provide the best camouflage and protection against predators. They emerge from the water as adults.

Caddis flies exhibit different life-styles and behaviours, especially as larvae. Some have adapted to scrape the surface of rocks under water; others are filter-feeders or predators. Among adults, some species are solitary, while others tend to aggregate. Caddis fly larvae require well-oxygenated water and are very sensitive to water pollution, which makes them ideal as indicators of water quality.

Alder-flies (Megaloptera)

There are about 300 species worldwide of alder-flies and the related dobsonflies. They have membranous wings with many veins and with their anterior pair slightly longer than the posterior. They are typically dark. The larva goes through ten larval stages, which last several years in total, until pupation, which takes place on land in moist soil beneath stones or wood. The pupa is alert and can defend itself against predators.

Snake flies (Raphidioptera)

The snake fly order contains 200 species in two families. Species from both families are characterized by an elongated head and prothorax (the foremost segment of the thorax which bears the first pair of legs) which allows the head to move rapidly for catching prey. Females have a long and slender ovipositor.

Snake flies are predatory as adults and larvae, feeding on aphids and other invertebrates. The female lays up to 800 eggs under bark in living or decaying trees, where the larvae actively hunt other arthropods. As with alder-flies, the pupa is rather active and mobile.

Lacewings (Neuroptera)

There are about 5,000 species of lacewings and relatives, and the order includes mantispids, owlflies, antlions and some other groups. There are 1,300 species of lacewings known, which makes theirs the largest family of the order. They are of moderate size with the largest species having a forewing length of 34mm (1.34in). As the name suggests, their wings have a delicate lace-like appearance. This family of insects is characterized by an auditory organ, which allows them to detect bat ultrasounds, as well as by their ability to communicate through vibration transmitted by moving the legs against the abdomen. The female lacewing lays about 300 eggs, commonly on stalks. Most larvae are brown with darker spots and markings and some cover themselves with the dried remains of their prey for camouflage. Their mouthparts are a pair of strong and long curved mandibles which they sink into the victim's body to suck out the body fluids. All larvae and adults feed on aphids and other soft-bodied insects, although some adults will also feed on honeydew.

Owlflies are large, often brightly coloured day-flying insects that hunt on the wing. Antlions are famous for their voracious larvae which trap ants and other insects in sandpits. Adult antlions look rather like dragonflies but are more delicate and have broader, blotched wings.

Below: Snake flies are most common in Europe, central Asia and North America. They are named for their elongated prothorax, which gives them a vaguely snake-like appearance.

Left: Caddis flies hold their hairy wings angled roof-like when at rest. They have the appearance of moths.

Above: Lacewings have chewing mouthparts and undergo complete metamorphosis.

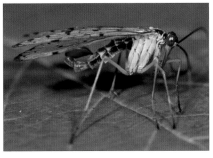

Above: Scorpion fly males are striking insects, with their scorpion-like tails and long, beak-like mouthparts.

Above: Female alder-flies lay thousands of eggs. The larvae are aquatic and have long filaments extending from the abdomen.

Scorpion flies (Mecoptera)

About 400 scorpion fly species are found around the world. They have a distinctive beak-like head with slender and serrated mandibles adapted for biting. Their abdomen is also elongated and in some males it ends in a scorpion-like tail, notably in members of the common scorpion fly family (Panorpidae). Unlike true scorpions, scorpion flies are harmless. They have membranous wings, which are often spotted, although some species are wingless. Most of the species are small, averaging 3mm (0.12in) but some can reach 30mm (1.18in). Scorpion flies are terrestrial either predatory (feeding on flies, aphids, caterpillars and moths), or scavengers or herbivores; some species prey on insects caught in spider webs.

Some scorpion flies display elaborate courtship behaviour. For instance, males offer a gift of prey before copulation to induce the female to mate or produce a column of saliva as a similar pre-copulatory gift.

Some species lay smooth and delicate eggs in crevices in small or large numbers, while others scatter their tougher eggs on the soil. Regardless of the species, the eggs generally require a moist environment from which they absorb water until they hatch. The larvae generally live in moist litter, feeding on dead insects or plants, especially mosses; some live in water and feed on live insects. Hanging scorpion flies also belong to this order. They look like craneflies and hang from a twig using their long forelegs.

Habitats of caddis flies, alder-flies, snake flies, lacewings and scorpion flies

Caddis flies have a largely aquatic lifestyle, spending most of their life in water as larvae and alongside streams or still waters as adults. The eggs, sometimes surrounded by a jelly-like substance, are laid underwater on the undersides of rocks. The larvae undergo up to seven different stages before the pupa, which is aquatic.

Snake flies are often found in the uppermost foliage of trees so are not very easy to spot. Adult females lay their eggs in cracks in the bark.

Alder-flies are found mainly in or around cool and well-oxygenated streams, but they also occur in standing waters. Females lay several thousand eggs on grass stems or other objects above water. After one to four weeks these hatch and fall into the water. The larvae are aquatic, living under stones or vegetation. They have strong, large mandibles adapted to catch other invertebrates, especially caddis flies. The adults do not feed.

Lacewings tend to live in forests but can be found in most of the habitats where aphids and their other prey exist.

Scorpion flies tend to live in habitats which provide them with shade and moisture, such as woodlands. They are often found living in mosses. Some species occur in arid regions but they are only active after rains. Antlions are found mainly in dry regions where their carnivorous larvae create sandpits to trap prey. Neuropterans generally are most diverse in the tropics.

BEETLES

The Coleoptera, or beetles, with more than 300,000 species and 166 families, constitute the largest order of insects. It has been estimated that one out of every five species of living organisms on the planet is a beetle. This order also has the largest families, with five containing more than 20,000 species.

Common features

Coleoptera means 'sheathed wing' (from the Greek: 'koleos' – sheath; and 'pteron' – wing). Beetles have two pairs of wings, but the first pair has been enlarged and thickened into a pair of hard sheaths, or elytra, which cover and protect the more delicate hindwings, as well as the dorsal surface of the abdomen. This distinctive feature has allowed beetles to exploit habitats such as leaf litter and the spaces under tree bark, and offers good protection to the wings. Although they have not adopted a truly aerial lifestyle, most beetles fly.

The mouthparts or mandibles are always of a biting type and resemble those of grasshoppers. They appear as large pincers on the front of some beetles. They are used to grasp, cut or crush prey or plant food.

Both the smallest and the largest of all insects can be found among this order, from the minute featherwing beetles (Ptiliidae), adults of which are just 0.25mm (0.01in) long, to the African Goliath and Hercules beetles (Scarabaeidae), measuring up to 15cm

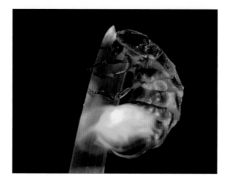

Above: Female glow-worms produce light to attract the winged males. The females retain a larva-like body form as adults.

Above: Click beetles have a mechanism which propels them into the air to escape predators, creating an audible click as they do so.

(6in) and weighing about 100g (3.5oz) true giants that are sometimes kept as unusual pets.

Beetles are exceedingly diverse ecologically and biologically. The majority of adult beetles are terrestrial herbivores, but several entire families and portions of others are predatory, fungivores or parasites, frequently with highly specialized life cycles and

Below: All beetles have claws to help them grip. They are visible on the feet of this stag beetle.

specific hosts. Though some beetles feed on nectar and pollen, this source has not been widely exploited by members of this order.

The typical life cycle of a beetle involves complete metamorphosis, from egg, through three to five larval stages, to pupa and adult. The length of the life cycle varies between species from a few weeks to many years. Some are known to spend decades as larvae.

Eggs can be laid either in clumps in substrates such as flour, or individually attached to leaves, or buried inside plant tissues. The typical larva is very voracious and usually the principal feeding stage of the beetle life cycle. Some feed on plants, but most feed on other insects. Although beetle larvae can be very diverse between species they are most often characterized by a hardened, dark head, the presence of chewing mouthparts and some openings along the sides of the body used for respiration.

Beetles provide some sort of parental care. Dung-beetles, for example, provide their young with food and shelter in the shape of a ball of dung.

Many beetle species are injurious to cultivated plants. Examples are the plum weevil or the grain weevils,

Above: Weevils are the most numerous of all beetles, accounting for around 20 per cent of beetle species.

Above: Beetles share the common feature of hardened wing cases, which protect the body of the insect.

Above: Some beetles meet and pair at flower-heads.

which live in nuts, fruits and grains and eat out the interior. The rice weevil (*Sitophilus oryzae*) and the granary weevil (*S. granarius*) are considered to be the most harmful weevils of all as they will attack all sorts of grains including rice, wheat and corn. Other beetles attack living conifer trees, such as the bark beetles of the family Scolytidae, causing damage to plantations.

On the other hand many beetle species play a beneficial role. Ladybirds are widely used for biological control, while glow-worm larvae eat snails and slugs. A few beetles are useful pollinators, while others, such as the dung-beetles, recycle animal wastes.

The following families include some of the most familiar and most numerous beetles in terms of species.

Weevils (Curculionidae)

Snout beetles or weevils are considered the most highly evolved family of Coleoptera. Containing more than 60,000 species worldwide, they comprise the largest single family in the animal kingdom. Weevils include some of the worst agricultural pests among insects.

Weevils have a distinctive long snout and clubbed antennae. Their form and size can vary greatly, with adult lengths ranging from 1–40mm (0.04–1.57in). Weevils are found on foliage or flowers as adults and are often spotted in gardens, but some species are ground dwellers or burrow in sand-dunes, and a few are aquatic or marine.

Adults are almost entirely herbivorous, feeding on seeds, fruits and other parts of plants, whereas the larvae are mostly internal plant feeders or subterranean. They are usually specialized to one species of plant.

Rove beetles (Staphylinidae)

Rove beetles are a large, varied family with very diverse modes of life; the number of species is estimated between 26,800 and 47,000. They often lurk around decaying matter.

These beetles are unusual in shape, with an elongated body and shortened elytra. Most groups have functional wings even though they are short in comparison to their body size. Some species typically run with their abdomen curled up, like scorpions. They are usually brown or black with a few species brightly coloured. Their size averages 1–10mm (0.04–0.39in) long.

Few species are herbivores. Most adults and larvae feed on invertebrates. Some feed on decaying vegetation.

Life cycle of a stag beetle

The stag beetle, *Lucanus cervus*, is typical for members of this order. The complete metamorphosis involves major changes in body shape from egg to adult. The larvae are soft-bodied grubs with hard, biting mouthparts.

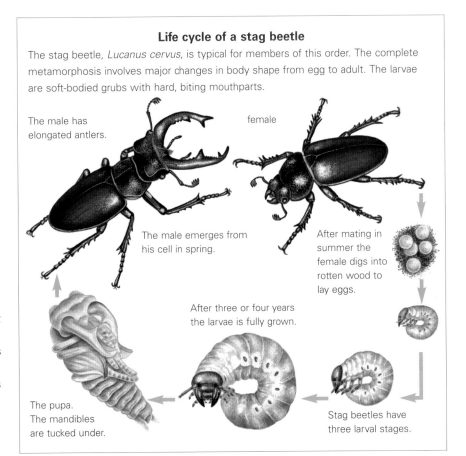

The male has elongated antlers.

female

The male emerges from his cell in spring.

After mating in summer the female digs into rotten wood to lay eggs.

After three or four years the larvae is fully grown.

The pupa. The mandibles are tucked under.

Stag beetles have three larval stages.

Above: Ladybirds, or ladybugs as they are known in North America, are among the best-loved beetles.

Above: Ladybird larvae, like the adults, are voracious predators of aphids, making them popular with gardeners.

Ground beetles (Carabidae)

Some of the world's best studied insects are ground beetles. They form a large and successful family with more than 40,000 named species.

They range from 1–60mm (0.04–2.36in) long. Most are flightless and if they have any wings, there are rather short and rarely used. Although around 30 per cent of species live in trees, these are predominantly ground-dwelling beetles. They are swift-running and active as adults.

Ground beetles are typically predatory and the majority of larvae have specific requirements as to the type of prey they will feed on. Some specialize in catching springtails, others in eating snails. A small percentage is herbivorous and some species feed exclusively on seeds.

Below: Many beetles are pests, destroying agricultural crops, while others are beneficial in a garden environment.

They are two types – the autumn breeders, which usually hibernate as larvae, and the spring breeders, which hibernate as adults. They usually lay eggs singly and deposit them on the ground or dig a small hollow. A few species construct mud or clay cells above the ground. Some species guard their eggs or store food for larvae. Most have three larval stages, a pupa and an adult stage.

Ground beetles can play a beneficial role in agriculture as they consume eggs of a range of pest insects, for example cabbage root-flies, cereal aphids and midges.

Scarab beetles (Scarabaeidae)

There are 27,800 species known worldwide in the scarab beetle family.

Most of the males are characterized by spectacular horns on the head used to fight over females. Scarab beetles have very diverse diets and feeding behaviour. Some larvae feed on rotting wood, others on mammal dung, carrion and roots of living vegetation. Certain beetles will choose a specific type of dung which they will provide to their larvae. Some will even tend the dung to prevent the growth of mould.

This family also contains the bulkiest of all beetles. Adults of some species such as the Japanese beetle *Popillia japonica* are significant pests as they attack living foliage, especially members of the rose family.

A few species are specialized as predators or cohabit in ant or termite nests. Scarabs range in size from burrowing species less than 20mm (0.79in) up to 10cm (4in) in length.

Longhorn beetles (Cerambycidae)

Longhorn beetles include more than 20,000 species, most of which have very long antennae. Some species resemble ants, bees or wasps and can be brightly coloured. The largest beetles from this family are found in the tropics, such as the 16cm- (6in-) long giant long-horned beetle (*Titanus giganteus*) from South America.

Most are associated with decaying woody plants but some can attack living trees. These beetles can cause serious damage to trees, as well as buildings made out of wood.

Darkling beetles (Tenebrionidae)

This is another large family with about 19,000 species. They are well represented in dry country, including deserts. They are highly variable in shape and size, ranging from 1–80mm (0.04–3.15in) long. They are often dark, but sometimes brightly coloured or metallic. They are often found on the ground under rocks and logs.

Jewel beetles (Buprestidae)

Characterized by their often dazzlingly bright colours, the jewel beetle family contains more than 14,000 species. The larvae are mostly wood-borers or leaf miners, with a few being considered as pests.

Below: Beetles have a wide and varied diet. A few species are reliant on a specific crop.

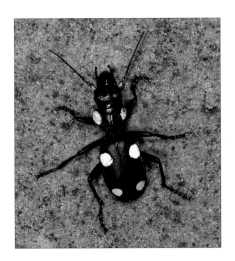

Above: Colouring can be a means of defence for a beetle.

Above: Beetles use their antennae to test and smell the environment around them.

Click beetles (Elateridae)

A family of around 10,000 species distributed worldwide. The click beetle name refers to a mechanism that creates a click and which allows the insects to fling themselves into the air if they are placed on their backs. The long cylindrical larvae are called 'wireworms' and are found in rotting wood. Many species feed on roots and can cause serious damage to crops. A few tropical species have bioluminescent spots.

Ladybirds (Coccinellidae)

This is one the most important families, as a majority of its species, known as ladybirds, feed on pest insects such as aphids and are widely used in biological control. However, some are also known to eat plants and crops and can be very destructive. There are around 5,000 species known.

These are small insects ranging from 1–10mm (0.04–0.39in). The most common species are yellow, orange or red with black spots. Most adults and larvae are predators on very small insects. A few species are plant eaters.

Most species breed in spring or summer and the female lays her eggs (from a few to hundreds) near aphid colonies. She sometimes lays infertile eggs as a provision for the young when food is scarce. The life cycle of a ladybird from egg to adulthood lasts four to seven weeks. The larva emerges from the egg within one to two weeks, and it then goes through four different larval stages and reaches maturity within two weeks. Pupation then takes place and the adults emerge after one or two weeks. Some species form aggregations as adults.

Water beetles (Dytiscidae)

This is the largest family of aquatic beetle, with about 4,000 species. The legs are modified as paddles for swimming. Body length ranges from 3–40mm (0.12–1.57in). These beetles typically hold air between the elytra and the abdomen when diving but they must periodically surface to renew their air supply, which restricts them to shallow water.

Most live in or near freshwater habitats. There are a few marine species, which tend to live on the shore.

Both adults and larvae are predatory; the larger species are able to kill small fish, although their main prey is tadpoles and invertebrates. The larvae in particular are voracious hunters, often known as 'water tigers'. The larvae breathe at the water surface through their tails and use their sharp jaws to catch their prey.

Habitats of beetles

Beetles exploit a variety of habitats throughout the world (except polar regions) from rainforest canopies and lakes to mountains and the driest deserts. As with most insects, they are most diverse in the tropics. They can also be found in deep caves and underground watercourses.

Rove beetles are found around decaying organic matter with a large number of species being associated with fungi, including moulds and rusts. Some have adapted to living in nests of social insects – mainly ants and termites – while others are found near water.

Ground beetles occupy every type of habitat from tropical rainforests, where they are found in the greatest numbers, to arid semi-deserts.

Scarab beetles inhabit burrows beneath their food source and come to the surface at night to feed.

Water beetles, as their name suggests, occupy many freshwater habitats.

FLIES

We see flies perhaps more than any other insects. Outdoors they are common and they are among the most visible and noisy creatures to enter our homes. As well as being a nuisance, some fly species carry diseases. A few, however, are beneficial to humans.

Common features

The order Diptera contains the insects commonly known as true flies. This is a large order with an estimated 85,000–100,000 species. Among the most common and familiar is the housefly, which has colonized every continent except Antarctica and is one of the world's most widely distributed animals.

They are mostly fairly small, with a single pair of functional wings, hence their scientific name Diptera (from the Greek 'di' – two, 'pteron' – wing). The second pair of wings is reduced. This feature distinguishes them from other insects also called flies. Although flies are predominantly aerial, about 20 families include members that are wingless or which have short wings. Some species belonging to the fungus gnat family are bioluminescent, producing their own light.

This is a diverse order with a wide range of ecological roles from herbivores and predators including the robber flies (Asilidae), to internal

parasites whose larvae develop inside a living host. Many, such as mosquitoes, are external parasites, feeding on blood, although the majority of the species feed on decaying organic matter, pollen or nectar. Some flies do not feed at all as adults.

Fly larvae also have an enormous variety of feeding habits. Many consume decaying organic matter, as seen in some mosquitoes and black flies, or are predacious; a large proportion are parasitic on other insects or organisms.

Left: Flies have large compound eyes and good eyesight, which they use to find food and avoid predators.

Life cycle

Diptera exhibit complete metamorphosis in their life cycle. Courtship and mating typically occurs in the air. Some courtship behaviours can be elaborate, such as in the dance flies, Empididae, where the male offers prey to the female. Eggs are usually small and deposited singly or in masses on or near the larval food. The larvae predominantly occur in moist to sub-aquatic habitats, and are often called maggots. They are commonly small, pale and soft-bodied. They lack true legs and have a reduced head. Adults have a short lifespan, from a few days to a few weeks.

Harmful species

Species such as the mosquitoes (Culicidae) are important as vectors of diseases including malaria, encephalitis and yellow fever, and can seriously affect humans and other animals. Black flies, deer flies and tsetse flies can also transmit diseases and house-flies can carry micro-organisms that cause dysentery. A few dipterans are pests of plants, such as root maggots, fruit flies, and leaf-mining flies, and these can seriously reduce crop yields.

Beneficial species

Perhaps surprisingly, some species can be useful. For instance, the vinegar fly *Drosophila melanogaster* has been widely used as an experimental subject in research into animal genetics and development. Other species are important pollinators, such as hover-flies. Some biting midges and sandflies are also important pollinators of tropical crops such as cacao. Overall, however, their contribution to pollination is rather small.

Habitats of flies

Dipterans have colonized most habitats and are widely distributed throughout the world. Very few species are restricted to one type of habitat or ecosystem. The majority of mosquito species live in the tropics. Midges are abundant in cooler climates. Many flies are attracted to rubbish and other waste, from which they pick up and carry disease. They are abundant in urban areas.

The larvae of some dipteran species help to provide clues in forensic science or are used in medicine to clean out wounds. Maggots are also bred commercially as bait for fishing, as well as food for captive reptiles or birds.

Some of the most important families of flies include the following.

Mosquitoes (Culicidae)

With about 1,600 species known, this family includes some important and familiar insects. They are typically slender flies, with piercing and sucking mouthparts.

Leatherjackets (Tipulidae)

Craneflies, or leatherjackets, are characterized by their large size and long legs. They are long and rather shapeless, with a sunken head. Some females can be wingless. Leatherjackets are plant root and foliage feeders.

Adults can occasionally feed on nectar or other fluids but generally do not feed. Larvae are usually found in damp soil where they feed on vegetation, mainly on plant roots, though some are scavengers and some are found in water.

A few craneflies, especially the larvae, are damaging to plants but they are otherwise harmless.

Deer or horseflies (Tabanidae)

There are about 3,500 species in this family. They are found in most of the world's ecosystems except in extreme northern and southern latitudes.

Adults feed on nectar and pollen, although females need to feed on blood for reproduction and their bites can be painful. The larvae are predatory and usually found in moist environments.

These are often considered as pests because of their bites. They can also transmit disease as well as parasites. Horseflies can cause severe damage to domesticated animals when abundant, causing some animals to lose up to 300ml (0.5 pint) of blood in one day. Some species are beneficial, especially in South Africa where they are important pollinators.

Large fruit flies (Tephritidae)

There are about 5,000 species of large fruit flies. These flies are among the most attractive and biologically interesting of the true flies, with patterned wings and often brightly coloured and patterned bodies. They also have elaborate behaviours both as adults and larvae.

Adults of many species may spend most of their life on one plant or adjacent plants of the same species. For example, the olive fruit fly feeds only on the fruit of cultivated olive

Below: All flies have just a single pair of wings. These are almost invariably transparent and point backward when the fly is at rest. Flies can land on almost any surface, including ceilings. Their feet secrete tiny droplets of slightly sticky fluid, which helps them to cling on.

Above: Craneflies have long, narrow wings and delicate dangling legs. Some craneflies can attain a length of 23cm (9in).

trees, and can ruin an olive crop. Tephritid larvae live in and feed on various plant tissues, depending on the species.

Most fruit flies lay their eggs in plant tissues, where the larvae will feed after emerging. The adults are particularly short-lived, some surviving less than a week.

Fruit flies are the most agriculturally significant family of flies. Some species are pests, causing major economic losses annually. Other species are beneficial biological control agents of weeds. Several species have been effective in destroying noxious weeds such as knapweeds.

Robber flies (Asilidae)

This family contains the robber-flies, with an estimated 4,000–7,000 species. They are moderate to large, and can be densely hairy. The family is characterized by the way they kill their prey, which are usually other insects caught in flight. They stab and inject their prey with saliva containing enzymes that paralyse the victim and enable it to be digested. These are active and powerful insects, often making rapid hunting forays from a perch.

Some species can cause economic damage by killing poultry, and some transmit worms causing diseases, such as *Onchocera volvulus*, which causes blindness in humans. They can also transmit encephalitis.

Flower- or hoverflies (Syrphidae)

This family has more than 5,000 species of colourful, moderate- to large-sized flies. The black-and-yellow coloration of many species often causes them to be confused with bees or wasps. However, their flight behaviour is quite distinctive and unlike that of wasps. Hoverflies dart quickly, then hover in one spot.

Agile in flight and often seen hovering, the adults are associated with flowers, of which they are important pollinators. The larvae, on the other hand, are variable in their feeding habits; some feed on plants, others on detritus or in aquatic habitats and many are important as predators of other insects. Some hoverflies are beneficial, feeding on aphids, scale insects and other pests. Others feed within the nests of social insects.

Gall midges (Cecidomyiidae)

These are very small flies, usually no longer than 2–3mm (0.08–0.12in), with many species being less than 1mm (0.04in) long. Their name refers to the larvae of most species, which feed within plant tissues, creating abnormal plant growths called galls, which provide shelter for the larvae. The number of species is estimated at 4,000.

Gall midges can reproduce before they reach the adult form, a rare phenomenon known as paedogenesis. Sometimes the larva gets eaten by its own progeny.

They are usually considered as pests and are especially injurious to wheat. However, a number of species, mainly at the larval stage, are beneficial to humans, as they naturally predate other crop pests such as aphids or spider mites. One species, *Aphidoletes aphidimyza*, is often used for biological control and is widely sold in the USA.

Above: Hoverflies are important pollinators of many flowers.

Black flies (Simulidae)

This family of 1,800 species is widely distributed worldwide. They are also known as buffalo gnats.

These flies are characterized by a stout body with short legs and an unusually pronounced curved thorax. The average size of most species is 2–5mm (0.08–0.19in) and wing length can vary from 1.5–6.5mm (0.06–0.26in). They can be black, grey or yellow.

The aquatic larvae are found in clean, fast-moving water of streams and rivers as well as in the shallows of large lakes.

Like mosquitoes, most species are blood feeders, although the males feed mainly on nectar.

Below: Gall midges and other insects cause unsightly marks on foliage.

Females deposit from 100 to 600 small, shiny, creamy-white eggs on water plants, rocks, twigs or leaves, in streams, or simply scatter the eggs over the water surface where they gradually sink. The eggs hatch in four to five days. Eggs deposited in the autumn do not hatch until the following spring when the water warms.

Young larvae attach themselves to submerged objects. Most species have six to nine larval stages. The larvae elongate with the hind part of their bodies swollen. Winter may be passed in the larval form.

Pupation occurs in a cocoon, under water. Adults emerge in a bubble of air, after two to three days, when the water is warm. They are capable of immediate flight and mating. The entire life cycle lasts about four to six weeks, depending on species, as well as on the water temperature and food availability. There can be four generations per year.

Females of certain species are blood feeders and can be a problem for people and animals. They are particularly difficult to control because they often occur in large swarms and can get into hair, eyes and nostrils.

FLEAS

Fleas belong to the order Siphonaptera. The order is entirely parasitic, with both adults and larvae spending their lives on the surface of vertebrate hosts. Adult fleas are laterally flattened and their back legs are very powerful for jumping on to their host.

Common features

This order contains the fleas, comprising 2,500 species distributed worldwide. The order name refers to their tube-like mouthparts 'siphon-' and the absence of wings '-aptera'. Fleas are highly specialized and unusual insects. External parasites, they feed on the blood of mammals and birds.

All flea species are small, measuring 1–5mm (0.04–0.19in) in length. They are dark coloured, with tube-like mouthparts adapted for piercing and sucking, and are covered with hairs and spines which project backward; these allow them to move more efficiently within hair or feathers. They are flattened laterally and wingless.

Habitats of fleas

Many fleas are mostly associated with a particular host, usually a mammal, but in some cases a bird. The adult fleas live in the fur or feathers, while the eggs and larvae develop in nests or bedding (or even in carpets).

Above: Some fleas are associated with a particular host. This is a hedgehog flea.

Fleas are agile insects with powerful hind legs adapted for jumping. Their body is tough and leathery, capable of withstanding great pressure so they cannot be killed easily. Flea larvae are worm-like and also covered with bristles. They lack eyes and have mouthparts adapted for chewing, and they have a pair of hook-like appendages on the last abdominal segment to attach more easily to their hosts.

Parasites

Adults feed on the blood of a wide variety of vertebrate animals but will usually parasitize animals that regularly return to their nests, bedding or burrows, such as rodents, bats or rabbits. They have not been observed on many animals that tend to have more nomadic behaviours, such as ungulates. More than 95 per cent of species are external parasites on mammals, with 74 per cent of fleas feeding on rodents; the remaining five per cent are parasites of birds.

Flea larvae feed on organic matter such as skin flakes and debris. As adults, they usually feed daily or every other day, but they can survive two months to a year without a blood meal. Females require more blood than the males, for the development of eggs.

Fleas are rarely species-specific and can have up to 35 different hosts, and a host can bear up to 22 different species of flea.

Fleas lay tiny eggs in batches of up to 20, usually on the host or nearby. The eggs take around two days to two weeks to hatch; the larvae are left in dark places to avoid sunlight and pupate within one or two weeks in a silken cocoon. After one or two weeks the adult is fully developed and ready to emerge. Adults usually live four to 25 days, although some have been known to live for a year. Female fleas can lay up to 1,000 eggs in a lifetime.

Fleas are a nuisance to their hosts and can provoke allergies. They also act as vectors of bacteria, protozoans and viruses. Rat-fleas can carry the organisms that cause diseases, such as plague and murine typhus, which have killed large numbers of people.

Below: Cat fleas are highly irritating to cats when they breed in large numbers. They can also bite humans.

BUTTERFLIES AND MOTHS

With their large, opaque wings, butterflies and moths are easy to spot in flight. The two are differentiated by their antennae and the way they hold their wings at rest. In addition to this, most moths are nocturnal, whereas butterflies are active by day. They both belong to the order Lepidoptera.

Common features

The order Lepidoptera, (meaning 'scale wings') is the second largest order of insects, with more than 200,000 species comprising moths and butterflies, which have distinctive life-styles and features. The moths include about 180,000 species and more than 120 families, compared with butterflies with some 20,000 species and five families.

This is not a very diverse order in terms of biology and morphology. Members of the group have overlapping rows of scales on the wings. The body and legs are also covered by similar scales or by long hair-like scales or bristles.

Members of certain species are flightless. Most, however, can fly. The majority of members of the order are moderate-sized, averaging about 30mm (1.18in) in wingspan. However, their sizes range from 2.5mm (0.09in) wingspan in pygmy moths up to 30cm (12in) among the emperor moths and some members of the swallowtails, such as Queen Alexandra's birdwing (*Ornithoptera alexandrae*).

The shape of the antennae differs between butterflies and moths. Butterflies have thread-like antennae with the tips thickened into knobs.

Moths have very diverse types of antennae, varying from filamentous and feathered to toothed or comb-like, depending on the species.

Feeding

Lepidoptera are mainly herbivorous insects. There are exceptions. One species of owlet moth is known to suck blood using a modified proboscis to penetrate the skin, and some other species do not feed at all and live on food reserves accumulated during their larval stage, their mouthparts having atrophied. Most of the adults, however, feed on nectar, honeydew or exudates from fermenting fruit or sap. Mouthparts typically form a tubular proboscis, used to suck up liquid food.

The larvae of most species are also herbivores, feeding on a wide range of plants, from roots to leaves. The larvae have chewing mandibles that allow them to feed on plants. Many feed on a single species of plant and most of these specialize on one part of the

Below: Male moths often have more elaborate antennae than females, using them to pick up pheromones and lead them to mates. The huge 'eyes' on the lower wings act as a deterrent to potential predators.

Above: Some caterpillars live in groups and construct silk tents for protection from predators.

plant such as the leaves, buds or wood. However, larval biology can be highly variable, including aquatic forms, borers in stems, seeds or fruit, gall-inhabiting forms, scavengers, and a few predators that feed on the eggs of spiders or other moths and butterflies.

Defence

To protect themselves from predators, butterflies and moths have developed various strategies. As a result the group displays great diversity of coloration and markings, which can serve for defence as well as for courtship. For example the wing patterns which resemble eyes of vertebrates, found in many species, are believed to have the effect of startling predators. Some butterflies, especially among the hairstreaks, use their hindwing tails as 'false heads' to confuse predators.

Some butterflies and moths have developed another kind of defence – mimicry. They mimic a poisonous or distasteful species which has a striking display of warning colours. For instance, some diurnal moths have

identical colour patterns to those of certain bees or wasps in order to dissuade predators from attack. Other species display bright colours to advertise the fact that they are poisonous themselves.

Just as adult butterflies and moths have warning colours, so do many larvae. Larvae and pupae also display cryptic patterns similar to the substrate on which they rest. It is particularly important for the chrysalis (pupa), which is quite vulnerable, to remain hidden. Caterpillars may also change colour in the course of their development.

Life cycle

All lepidopterans have a complete, holometabolous (complete metamorphosis) life cycle, with egg, larva, pupa and adult stages.

Eggs are deposited on the host plant, or into the plant tissues, either singly or in groups. The total number laid can vary from a dozen to more than 18,000, with an average of 100–200 eggs; as many as 50,000 eggs have been recorded among some ghost moth females.

Some species, mainly moths, pupate on the host plant in a silken cocoon, within their leaf mine or in leaf rolls. Others pupate in the soil or leaf litter such as hawk moth larvae, which make an underground pupal cell.

Below: Butterflies at rest hold their wings closed together. The undersides are often less brightly coloured than the upper sides.

Life cycle of a red admiral butterfly

Known in many parts of the world, the red admiral butterfly, *Vanessa atalanta,* is one of the largest and most beautiful of predominantly European butterflies. It is brighter in coloration in the summer months and can vary in size depending on location. This butterfly is 'people-friendly' and will perch on a human.

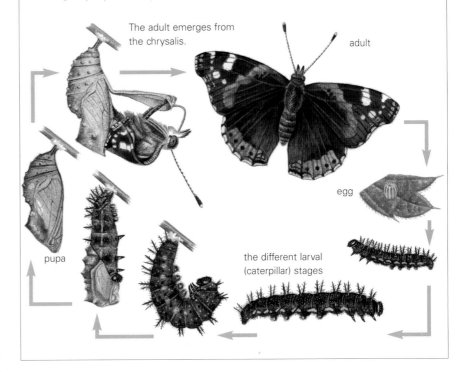

The adult emerges from the chrysalis.

adult

egg

pupa

the different larval (caterpillar) stages

Many butterflies hang head-down as a chrysalis (pupa) in a membranous covering. Depending on the species, the pupal stage may last from a few days to several years. Overall, most species have a short lifespan.

Some species are well known for their migratory behaviour, such as the well-studied monarch butterfly. The species migrates and aggregates in autumn to overwintering sites before dispersing and reproducing the following spring. Aggregation can also occur at night in some species, which is believed to be defensive behaviour against predation, for example in *Heliconius* butterflies. Other species hibernate in winter as adults.

Harmful species

Some species of moths and butterflies are known for the severe damage they cause to crops as caterpillars. The rice and grain moths (Pyralidae) cause damage to stored grain. Some also attack horticultural plants. Clothes moths, Tineidae, whose larvae can

make holes in blankets, clothes and carpets, can be a real nuisance in the home. A few species are beneficial, including *Cactoblastis cactorum*, which has been used in Australia to control the invasive prickly pear cactus, *Opuntia*.

Below: A monarch butterfly feeds on a flower. Both butterflies and moths have long, tubular mouthparts for drinking nectar.

Butterflies

The largest families of butterflies, the Nymphalidae and Lycaenidae each have about 6,000 species. One of the best known is the swallowtail family (Papilionidae) with about 600 species. The skippers (Hesperiidae) number about 3,500 species, and the whites and relatives (Pieridae) about 1,000.

Brush-footed butterflies (Nymphalidae)

This family includes well-known species such as the fritillaries, admirals, emperors, monarchs and tortoiseshells. They vary considerably in their appearance but are generally characterized by reduced and hairy front legs. Their caterpillars also vary, but are often hairy or spiny.

Many species are brightly coloured, but the undersides of the wings are generally duller, which helps the butterfly to escape detection by predators.

Lengthy migrations, territoriality and the ability to overwinter as adults have been observed in many members.

Blues, coppers and relatives (Lycaenidae)

This family contains about 40 per cent of all butterfly species. Adults usually have wingspans less than 50mm (2in).

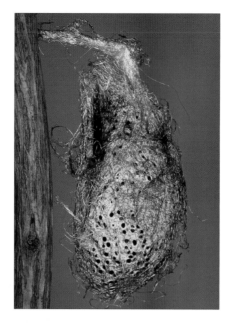

Above: These insects are hanging inside a hardened case, or chrysalis, as they metamorphose from caterpillar to adult.

They are brightly coloured, sometimes metallic, with blue and copper being the predominant colours. Larvae are more flattened than cylindrical.

Most species are herbivores but some species feed on aphids or ants.

About 75 per cent of lycaenid species have developed a strong relationship with ants, which can be parasitic, predatory or mutualistic.

In the latter, both species benefit. The larvae are tended and protected by the ants, which receive in return a sugar-rich honeydew produced by the larvae. Some species can complete their life cycle only in the presence of ants.

Swallowtail butterflies (Papilionidae)

The swallowtails and their relatives are among the most specialized lepidopterans in terms of behaviour and ecology. The name swallowtail refers to the extensions commonly found at the tips of the hindwings, although this feature is not present in all species. Many of them are large and colourful. Because of this, many swallowtail species have been collected for displays and their wings used in jewellery. Some have therefore become rare.

Powerful in flight, using alternating periods of flapping and gliding, swallowtails can cover large distances as they search for food or breeding sites. The caterpillars can easily be distinguished from those of other families thanks to the presence of a fork-like organ behind their head which can emit smelly secretions as a defence against predators. The pupae hang upside down using a hook called a 'cremaster', located on the rear of the chrysalis, another typical feature of the Papilionidae. This family includes large, magnificent birdwings.

Moths

The largest and best-known families of moths are the Noctuidae with about 26,000 species, the Arctiidae with over 11,000 species and the Tortricidae with about 9,000 species.

Owlet moths (Noctuidae)

Species belonging to the Noctuidae family occur worldwide. They have a robust appearance, a medium size and dull colours, although some species have brightly coloured hindwings. Some species that are highly predated by bats have developed a tiny ear-like

Left: Most moths have opaque wings but in a few species they are clear. Almost all moths, like butterflies, feed on nectar.

Above: Butterflies and moths lay their eggs directly on the species of plants on which their larvae feed. Many are confined to just one plant type.

organ which can detect the ultrasounds emitted by their hunters.

Noctuid caterpillars frequently hide under debris or leaf litter, emerging at night to feed. They often chew through stems, hence their common name 'cutworms'. Some species are serious horticultural and agricultural pests.

Woolly bears (Arctiidae)

The family name Arctiidae comes from the Greek 'arctos', meaning bear, referring to the hairy appearance of these caterpillars, which are popularly known as woolly bears or woolly worms. A large and diverse family, arctiids are found virtually everywhere in the world, but are most common in the tropics. The family includes the brightly coloured tiger moths, but also footmen, which are much duller, lichen moths and wasp moths. Like owlet moths, arctiids are sensitive to bat sonar. Uniquely they can produce ultrasonic sounds, which are used in mating and defence against predators; these can interfere with the ultrasounds emitted by bats, which then have difficulties locating their prey. Many species retain distasteful or poisonous chemicals obtained from the plants they fed on as caterpillars. Others produce their own chemicals. These defences are generally advertised with bright coloration, unusual postures or odours. Some arctiid caterpillars have adapted to cold temperatures by producing a protectant chemical – a sort of natural antifreeze. Many adults and larvae are active during the day.

Leaf-roller moths (Tortricidae)

This family contains the leaf-roller moths. Most of the adults are small, from 8–30mm (0.31–1.18in) in wing-span, and the caterpillars are generally smooth-skinned. Some species have particular distinguishing features, such as the bell moths whose name refers to the shape of the adult when at rest. Others have a striking resemblance to bird droppings, which helps to camouflage them from predators.

The caterpillars typically roll the leaves in which they pupate, hence the common name. Some species drop on a silken thread when disturbed. The famous Mexican jumping bean is caused by the movement of the larva of the tortricid moth *Cydia deshaisiana* which lives inside seeds.

Some species feed destructively on plants and can be of considerable economic significance, such as the

Above: Many moths are beautifully patterned and coloured, but are difficult to spot on some surfaces.

spruce budworm, *Choristoneura fumiferana*, and the fruit-tree roller, *Archips argyropsilus*. Others are leaf miners or feed on dead leaves on the forest floor. Many larvae bore into fruit, nuts or seeds and can cause severe damage. The larvae are a favourite food of many birds.

Habitats of butterflies and moths

Butterflies and moths have colonized most habitats, from the Arctic to the tropical jungles. Specially adapted to feed from flowers, butterflies are associated with rich meadows, woodland and forest clearings, and other sites where there are vegetation and flowers. They are also very welcome colourful visitors to parks and gardens. They can be found on every continent except Antarctica. They are most diverse in the tropics, but are also common in temperate regions.

The largest number of species is found in east and South-east Asia.

BEES, WASPS, PARASITIC WASPS, ANTS, SAWFLIES AND WOOD WASPS

This large order, known as Hymenoptera, contains many insect species that live highly social lives, often in large colonies. Their wings are thin and transparent and many species can deliver poisonous stings. Many species are important pollinators of flowers and crops.

Common features

Hymenoptera is the third largest order of insects, with more than 280,000 species. It includes the familiar wasps, bees and ants, as well as the rather less familiar sawflies, wood wasps and parasitic wasps (including ichneumons). It is a diverse group well known for the advanced social behaviour of some of its members, often involving separate reproductive and worker castes, as well as the complicated forms of communication displayed by some species.

Hymenopterans are characterized by their membranous wings, which has given the name to the group, derived from the Greek 'hymen' – membrane, and 'pteron' – wing. They usually have two pairs of wings. Members of

Right: Bees ingest nectar through a straw-like proboscis. Flowers produce nectar specifically to attract bees and other pollinating insects.

certain species, notably ants, only have wings at specific stages of their life cycle.

Hymenopterans have a very mobile head with well-developed mandibles adapted for chewing, as well as for attacking or defending themselves. In most species the mandibles are more often used for cutting the insect's way out of the pupal case or for nest-building rather than for feeding. However, a worker ant may dig, transport food or soil particles, manipulate prey, defend the colony, or tend grubs, all using the mandibles.

The morphological adaptations most responsible for the success of bees and wasps involve the abdomen, with the presence of a long tube called the 'ovipositor' (egg-laying tube). This has developed as a piercing organ, which can be inserted deeply into plant or animal tissues to deposit the eggs. In some it is modified into a sting; this adaptation provides efficient protection against predators. The larvae of hymenopterans are mostly grub-like. The pupae may grow in cocoons or in special cells, or develop inside the host in parasitic forms.

Bees (superfamily Apoidea)

There are more than 20,000 species of bee, found on every continent except Antarctica, and in every habitat that contains flowers. Bees have a long tube-like organ or proboscis which allows them to obtain nectar from flowers. Adults range in size from about 2–40mm (0.08–1.57in).

Bees are divided into two types: solitary bees and social bees. In solitary species, adults construct individual nests and provide their young with plant materials, usually nectar or pollen. They rear their young in the nest but do not produce honey or wax. Social bees by contrast build

Life cycle of a blue carpenter bee

The blue carpenter bee, *Xylocopa violacea*, is a solitary bee. Like many bees these insects dig nests underground.

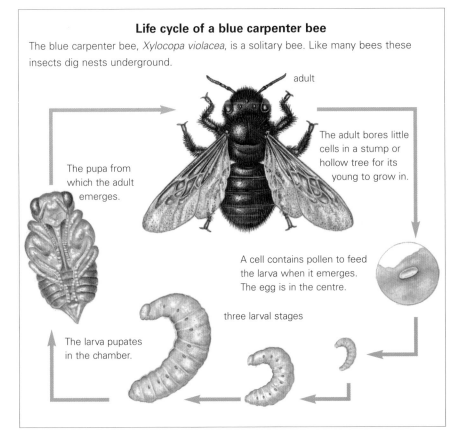

adult

The adult bores little cells in a stump or hollow tree for its young to grow in.

The pupa from which the adult emerges.

A cell contains pollen to feed the larva when it emerges. The egg is in the centre.

three larval stages

The larva pupates in the chamber.

communal nests in the soil (typical of bumblebees) or in cavities (honey bees). They belong to one large family (Apidae) and they are among the most familiar and well studied insects. There are two levels of sociality among social bees. Some are 'semi-social' with groups of sisters cohabiting and dividing labour between them. Others show a higher level of sociality and are called 'eusocial'. Eusocial species are characterized by the presence of a queen which gives birth to sterile females, commonly called workers. These carry out specialized tasks among the colony. Eusociality can itself be divided into a primitive form, where queens and workers are very similar and the colony relatively small, and a more evolved form where the different castes differ morphologically and the colony can contain up to 40,000 individuals.

Their strict diet of pollen and nectar makes bees very important in agriculture and horticulture worldwide. Honey bees and bumblebees will fly from flower to flower to collect nectar and pollen, using their long proboscis, and these

Above: As well as drinking nectar, bees sometimes collect pollen to feed to their young, carrying it in bundles on their back legs.

Above: Bumblebees have more rounded, hairy bodies than honey bees, wasps or hornets.

foods are then converted to honey to feed the larvae. During the process, the pollen remaining on the insect is transported from one flower to another and pollination may occur if a subsequent flower the bee lands on is of the same species.

Wasps (superfamilies Vespoidea and Sphecoidea)

Classification of wasps is quite complex, and includes solitary as well as social species. The following are some of the important groups.

Parasitic wasps (division Parasitica)

This group contains fig wasps and gall wasps and related hymenopterans, including ichneumons and braconids. There are 200,000 species. Many are black or yellow, with transparent wings and are rather small, averaging 1.5mm (0.06in) in length. The larvae are parasitic on other insects. The adults mainly feed on plant nectar.

Hunting wasps (Vespidae)

These are either solitary or social species that mainly catch their prey by stinging and paralysing it. This group includes common wasps ('yellow jackets'), hornets and paper wasps, as well as some solitary wasps.

Most social wasps are fairly large and there are about 5,000 species found throughout the world. A typical colony includes a queen and a number of sterile female workers. In temperate climates, colonies typically last one year, dying when winter comes. New queens and males are produced at the end of the summer, and after mating the queen hibernates over winter in sheltered locations, starting a new colony the following spring. The nests are made out of plant fibres which are chewed to make a kind of paper, hence the name 'paper wasps'. Prey are chewed before being fed to larvae, and the larvae in return produce a liquid consumed by adults.

Below: Wasps guard the entrance to their nest. The nest appears to have a paper-like quality.

Ants (family Formicidae)

The Formicidae are one large family of ants containing 14,000 species. The family name refers to the formic acid that ants naturally produce to defend themselves. Most ants are relatively small 2–25mm (0.08–1in), but the queens can be sizeable insects. The queens of one species, *Dorylus helvolus*, from southern Africa, grows up to 50mm (2in) long, making them the world's biggest ants. Most ant larvae are grub-like: their heads are extremely reduced and they lack legs. As such, they are completely helpless and rely on the worker ants entirely to feed them and to move them around.

Ants are highly social insects. Their colonies can consist of millions of individuals divided into castes or social groups, including sterile female workers, fertile males and fertile female queens. Each colony has at least one queen. The queens are the only individuals to lay eggs, which are then looked after by the workers. The different castes show a more or less wide range of morphological differences, depending on the species.

The lifespan of ants varies among the castes, with sterile females living from one to three years, whereas

Below: Worker ants carry partly developed larvae to safety, after their nest has been disturbed.

queens can live up to 30 years. Males usually only survive a few weeks. Colonies are large, and those of some tropical army ants may number several million individuals.

Ants are characterized by their organized permanent colonial life and their advanced social behaviour. They co-operate to an amazing extent, gathering food and hunting in large masses, even using their own bodies as bridges for other ants of the colony. Ants communicate through chemicals, which produce behavioural changes in other individuals.

Most ant species have also developed specific behaviours, some of which are strongly associated with plants. The leaf-cutter ants, for example, behave rather like farmers harvesting pieces of leaves and carrying them back to the nest (they can lift up to 20 times their own body weight). The leaves are then chewed to allow a fungus, on which the ants feed, to grow on them. Ants can also be pollinators, or protectors of plants. Some ant species in Africa live on acacia trees (in galls produced by the tree's tissues) and their presence on the twigs and branches helps to defend those trees against attack from giraffes and other herbivores.

Slave-maker ants raid the nests of other ants to steal their pupae, which are then used as slaves in the colony after they hatch.

Above: This ants' nest, built in Kenya, has become a large structure. These structures are common and litter the landscape in certain areas.

Various types of nests can be found among the different species, from the 'bivouac' type formed by the ants' own bodies observed in nomadic species such as army or driver ants, to the sophisticated leaf nests built in trees by weaver ants, or large colonies in mounds or under the soil.

Sawflies and wood wasps (suborder Symphyta)

These are considered the most primitive of all Hymenoptera, partly as they do not show the complex social behaviour observed in many other groups. They are widespread, with about 10,000 species. Their common name refers to the ovipositor, which has the appearance of a saw blade, being toothed along one edge.

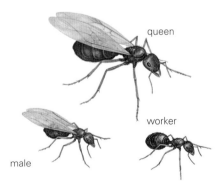

Above: Only male ants and queens have wings and these are just for the nuptial flight, when they meet and mate.

Above: Adult sawflies can fly well, but often prefer to clamber about on leaves or flowers.

A number of sawflies are considered to be pests, boring into wood or defoliating plants. Wood wasps have sturdy ovipositors and can use these to drill into timber.

Adults mostly have a dark body and legs, and look rather like wasps or flying ants. However, they lack the narrow 'waist' of most hymenopterans. The larvae look like caterpillars in general appearance and are often camouflaged in shades of green.

These hymenopterans are characteristically external foliage feeders and affect a number of different plants, depending on the species. Some feed on herbs or ferns, but most feed on trees and shrubs. Among the most common are the apple sawfly, the common gooseberry sawfly and the pear and cherry slugworm. Adults of some species are carnivorous or feed on nectar. Some of the larvae are internal feeders including leaf miners and gall formers, and are generally legless.

Adult sawflies generally do not live for more than two weeks. In many species, flower pollen forms a major part of their diet. Eggs are deposited in slits made in leaves or pine needles, and the mature larvae usually leave the host plant to pupate in a cocoon or in a cell in soil or leaf litter.

Right: An ants' nest has been carefully constructed of leaves.

Habitats of ants

Many ants nest underground, so that even where they are common they remain largely hidden. An ants' nest is made up of many different chambers. In forests they recycle huge amounts of material and in tropical rainforests in particular they play a major role in maintaining the stability of the immediate ecosystem in which they live.

Ants are common in both temperate and tropical parts of the world. Wood ants build large domed nests from pine needles. Often, as here, their nests are sited over a decaying tree stump, which provides heat as well as structure. Inside they have many different chambers used by different members of the colony.

MILLIPEDES AND CENTIPEDES

Millipedes (about 11,000 species) and centipedes (about 3,000 species) are the main classes in the superclass Myriapoda – many-legged arthropods – which has about 15,000 species in total. The other two myriapod classes are the symphylans (about 200 species) and the pauropods (about 700 species).

Millipedes (Diplopoda)

The name millipede is misleading as these creatures never have more than 350 pairs of legs. In fact, most millipedes have fewer than 50 pairs of legs. Millipedes vary in size and shape, some being long and flat-bodied, others are short with bristle-like hairs or prominent lateral projections. Some, such as the pill millipede resemble woodlice and can protect themselves by rolling into a tight ball. Millipedes have rather hardened heads, which helps them move through rotting wood or compacted soil. Adults vary from 2–30cm (0.08–12in) in length, and in colour from whitish to brown or black. They can secrete toxic chemicals through glandular openings on each side of each body segment, and this helps protect them from predators such as spiders and ants.

With elongated, segmented bodies like their close relatives the centipedes, millipedes differ from centipedes in having two pairs of legs on most body segments instead of one. In comparison they are slower-moving creatures.

Millipedes feed mainly on dead plant material, usually leaf litter, but they occasionally eat seeds as well as roots and shoots of seedlings; some species are scavengers. They tend to wait until leaves are partially degraded before they feed on them.

The millipede life cycle is rather long compared with that of other arthropods. It can take from one to four years before millipedes complete their metamorphosis. Sperm is transferred from the male to the female by means of specially adapted legs. The eggs are deposited in spring or summer, in a cluster in the soil, sometimes in a chamber or cell. Females lay between 50 and 300 eggs, which hatch within nine or ten days. The larva looks like the adult except it only has a few segments and three pairs of legs. Body segments are added at each moult. Millipedes usually go through ten different larval stages or moults. Parthenogenesis occurs in some species.

Some millipedes can be a pest in the garden or greenhouse, such as the garden millipede *Oxidus gracilis*, introduced to temperate areas from the tropics. The spotted millipede is another pest, feeding on bulbs and roots of vegetables.

Millipedes, however, are of ecological importance, as decomposers recycling organic matter. In some habitats they ingest more than ten per cent of the annual leaf litter.

Above: Many millipedes coil up if threatened, protecting their legs and leaving just their smooth, rounded sides exposed.

Centipedes (Chilopoda)

Most centipedes move more quickly, being active hunting carnivores. They have colonized diverse habitats in many parts of the world.

Centipedes measure from 1–10cm (0.5–4in) in length on average, but some species such as the Amazonian giant centipede *Scolopendra gigantea* can reach 30cm (12in). They have long bodies but only a single pair of legs per body segment instead of the two pairs characteristic of millipedes. Many species have 15 pairs of legs, but some, such as *Gonibregmatus plurimipes*, a species found in the Pacific islands, have as many as 191 pairs. Centipedes are adapted for running and are fast. Some of the largest species have longer legs toward the end of the body, which enhances their speed. Some soil-dwelling species move by coiling their body in a worm-like movement, as well as using their legs. Centipedes have a unique adaptation in which the legs of the first body segment have been modified into claws containing poison glands; this allows them to kill their prey efficiently, as well as to defend themselves.

Below: Millipedes and centipedes are long and slender multi-legged insects that are immediately identifiable.

Right: Millipedes have long legs which stick out from the sides of their bodies.

Centipedes are predatory, feeding on insects, snails and earthworms. The largest species can feed on rodents, toads or even snakes. They use their antennae and legs to find their prey, which is then killed using their poison-bearing jaw-like claws.

Centipedes reproduce externally, the male depositing its spermatozoa in a small web, which is then taken up by the female. Reproduction is sometimes preceded by a courtship dance, depending on the species, and generally occurs in spring and summer in temperate regions. Some species lay a single egg in a hole, others lay between 15 and 60 eggs in a nest located in the soil or in rotten wood. The latter tend to show parental care as they guard and lick their eggs to prevent fungi growing on them and protect them against predators. In some species the female guards the young until they leave the nest. Many species are known to have five or six different larval stages and reach the adult stage within one to three years. The young have seven pairs of legs on hatching and develop the rest of the segments and legs with successive moults. Most species live for three to six years.

Some species can be venomous and although they are not lethal to humans they can cause severe irritation and damage to the skin. Large centipedes are best treated with respect.

Below: Leaf litter provides a hunting ground for centipedes and food for millipedes.

Habitats of millipedes and centipedes

Woodland vegetation provides an ideal millipede habitat, with plenty of decomposing plant matter for them to burrow under.

Millipedes are usually found under leaf litter or stones, or below the surface in moist environments such as deciduous forests, as many species are sensitive to desiccation. Some, such as the black millipedes, are known to climb trees. A few occur in very dry environments such as deserts, or at high altitude. Some species have developed strong relationships with ants, where the ants provide protection and the millipedes help to clean up detritus from the nests. Other millipede species form associations with termites.

Centipedes live in terrestrial habitats, either in soil, under leaf litter or beneath stones and bark, and are active mainly at night. Unlike millipedes, they tend to live in dry and arid environments including deserts, though some species require a humid environment. A few are found near the sea, among seaweeds.

SPIDERS, MITES AND TICKS

Arachnids are one of the largest groups of predatory arthropods. The most familiar are the spiders; these and the mites and ticks each have about 35,000 species. The other main arachnid groups are scorpions (about 1,500 species), pseudoscorpions (about 2,000 species) and harvestmen (about 4,500 species).

Common features

Arachnids have distinctive features that differentiate them from insects. These include a two-segmented body, four pairs of walking legs (although some mites can have fewer), and no antennae or wings. They also have simple rather than compound eyes. The number of eyes varies from none to as many as 12 in some scorpions.

Apart from some mites and the water spider (*Argyroneta aquatica*), most arachnids are terrestrial. They are mainly carnivorous, feeding on insects and other small animals.

The reproductive behaviour is unusual in many species, with prolonged and complex courtship. Parental care is common among spiders. Arachnids usually lay eggs, which hatch into offspring that look like miniature adults.

The class Arachnida consists of 11 subclasses, of which the five included here are the largest and by far the best known.

Spiders (Aranae)

Spiders produce silk, which emerges from the tip of the abdomen. Silk is very strong and flexible and is used by spiders for many purposes, including spinning webs. Most spiders have

Below: A spider clutches her egg cocoon close to her body.

Above: This spider, like many, is very well camouflaged.

Above: Spiders spin webs in which to trap their prey.

poison glands, but they are not all dangerous. The majority of species have eight eyes, arranged in two rows.

There are 35,000 species of spider in more than 100 families. Major groups include the tiny money spiders; orb-weaving spiders; wolf spiders; crab spiders; jumping spiders; trap-door spiders; and the large tarantulas.

Although a few include pollen in their diet, most spiders are carnivores. Most spiders are generalist predators. Prey are usually smaller or similar in size, but many spiders can subdue prey which are several times their own weight. Some spiders will occasionally feed on vertebrates. A few scavenge dead insects. Some spiders stalk their prey, others ambush it, while a few species steal prey captured by other spiders. Most trap their prey in some kind of web. Spiders paralyse their victims by injecting poison secreted by a pair of poison glands in the front jaws.

Female spiders lay their eggs within a few weeks of mating, usually placing them in a silken sac for protection.

Most female spiders can produce multiple egg sacs, each containing from a few to more than 1,000 eggs. In many species, the female guards the egg sacs against predators until hatching, which usually takes a few weeks. In a few species she provides food for her offspring. After one or two weeks the young are ready to disperse. In temperate regions, most species live for one or two years. Some of the longest-lived spiders are female tarantulas, which may live for up to 25 years, (the males rarely live for more than a couple of years).

Mites and ticks (Acari)

Mites and ticks are a large and diverse group of mostly very small arachnids. They greatly outnumber all other arachnids and are distributed worldwide. There are more than 34,000 named species of mites and about 850 species of tick. They vary in length from 1–7mm (0.04–0.28in) for mites and from 2–30mm (0.08–1.18in) for ticks. Their two-part body is fused into one piece. Although adults of most species have four pairs of legs some have fewer, and the larval stages of many species have only three pairs. Most larvae have six legs, as opposed to eight at the nymphal and adult stages. Some mites can produce silk in their palps. Mites and ticks are the most common external parasites of humans and other vertebrates.

Mites and ticks pass through at least four life stages – egg, larva, nymph and adult – but there is a great deal of variation, often including extra stages. A moult occurs between each stage.

Mites

Free-living and parasitic mite species exist, with the free-living being the most common. Parasitic species attack both vertebrates and invertebrates, causing damage by burrowing under skin. Other species live in or near the hair follicles of mammals including humans. The best-known mite is the house dust mite, associated with asthma. Bees and other insects are commonly attacked by mites.

Many mites cause damage to crops and stored products, and can also be vectors of important diseases of humans and domestic animals. Some species are of ecological importance and are a key element within eco-systems as decomposers, in breaking down leaf litter to produce humus.

Ticks

Soft and hard ticks exist. Both types are exclusively blood-feeding, on vertebrates. Soft ticks typically live in

---

Life cycle of a Mexican red-kneed tarantula

The bird-eating Mexican red-kneed tarantula, *Brachypelma smithii,* is a common pet. The young spider emerges from the egg and is a miniature version of the adult it will become. The female spider can live for 25 years.

It can take up to five years to reach full maturity.

The adult female lays 100–400 eggs.

The female stays close to the egg sac.

Young spiders moult several times a year.

Young spiders remain in the nest after hatching.

---

crevices and emerge briefly to feed, whereas hard ticks attach themselves to the skin of a host for a long period.

Harvestmen (Opiliones)

Like spiders, harvestmen (or harvest spiders) have jaws and pedipalps at the front, and four pairs of walking legs. The two parts of the body are broadly joined so that they appear to be just one piece. They only have two eyes and do not produce silk, neither do they have poison glands, although they

do have defensive glands on each front leg that produce an odorous and distasteful fluid. They are all moderately large with a body size up to 10mm (0.39in), and are more or less brownish in colour.

Most harvestmen are nocturnal and feed on a variety of other arthropods and invertebrates, including other arachnids, insects, woodlice, small snails and earthworms. Dead and faecal material may also be eaten. They also feed on plant matter,

---

Below: Red velvet mites are large by mite standards.

Below: Ticks are small and have rather hard, flattened bodies.

Below: Beetles are sometimes infested with parasitic mites.

but mainly for its water content. They drink from dewdrops on vegetation.

Harvestmen typically live for one year, usually passing the winter as eggs and maturing in late summer. The female harvestman uses her ovipositor to lay up to 100 eggs in damp soil.

Scorpions (Scorpiones)

Scorpions are rather large arachnids, ranging from 4–17cm (1.5–7in) long. They do not possess silk glands, but typically have a sting at the end of a long, upcurved tail, used both to subdue large prey and in defence.

While many are harmless, some are mildly toxic, and a handful are dangerous, able to inflict a lethal sting. There are several deadly species which possess highly potent neurotoxins. These include the fat-tailed scorpion, *Androctonus australis*, of Africa and Asia, which can kill an adult human within four hours. Dangerous scorpions are also found in South America, the Middle East and Africa.

Scorpions have poor eyesight and are primarily nocturnal. Like most arachnids, scorpions are predators. They use claw-like

Above: These relatives of spiders are less numerous and less often seen. Like spiders they are all predators and most count insects among their prey.

pedipalps to capture and hold their prey while stinging it with their barb-tipped abdomen.

Courtship in scorpions is complex and can last for hours or even days. The pair grasp each other's pincers and circle in a kind of dance. This is to move the female over the spermatophore (packet of sperm) that the male has deposited. The fertilized eggs develop within the female, which gives birth to live young. The baby scorpions climb on to the female's abdomen and are carried about until their first moult, after which they typically disperse. Scorpions may live for several years, even after reaching adulthood. Some species have been recorded as living for up to 20 years – nearly as long as tarantulas.

Pseudoscorpions (Pseudoscorpiones)

These creatures resemble miniature scorpions, but lack the arching, stinging tail. Few are larger than 5mm (0.19in) and they generally average 2–4mm (0.08–0.16in) in length. They are characterized by a flat, segmented

---

Habitats of spiders, mites and ticks

Spiders inhabit nearly every part of the world, from polar to tropical regions. They are particularly abundant in areas of rich vegetation.

Harvestmen are commonly found in hedgerows, parks and gardens, on tree trunks, walls and fences.

Mites and ticks have colonized nearly every ecosystem, including marine and freshwater. Unlike other arachnids, many are highly specialized, including a number of species which are parasitic on plants and animals, and a few which are exclusively aquatic. Some live in moss and leaf litter, feeding on fungus and mould. Ticks are often found in tall grass,

shrubs or trees where they will wait to attach or drop on to passing hosts.

Scorpions typically live in hot, dry climates, but they can also be found in tropical and subtropical forests, on high mountains, in grassland, caves, intertidal zones and other habitats. In deserts they survive by spending the day under rocks or in deep burrows, and only come out at night to feed and mate.

Pseudoscorpions are commonly found in moss, leaf litter, and the top layers of the soil, as well as under stones. Some live in very specialized habitats, such as under the wing cases of beetles, where they prey on mites.

abdomen, four pairs of short, pale legs and long pedipalps, with terminal pincers held out in front. Some species have poison glands in their pincers, which they use to capture small insects.

Most pseudoscorpions have one or two pairs of eyes on the side of the carapace, although some have none. The body colour ranges from yellowish to dark brown, with the pincers sometimes black. The body and appendages are sparsely covered with tactile hairs used to detect prey and predators. Pseudoscorpions produce silk from the pincers of the pedipalps, which is used for making chambers for moulting, overwintering, and brooding the young.

Pseudoscorpions are carnivorous, actively hunting for their prey, which they catch using their pincer-like pedipalps. Pseudoscorpions are beneficial as they commonly feed on pest species such as clothes moth larvae, ants, mites and small flies.

Courtship is similar to that of the scorpions, but unlike scorpions, they produce eggs which remain in a small sac held below the abdomen of the female. The larvae stay in the sac to be nourished by a milk-like secretion from the mother's ovaries. When they leave

Below: Like spiders, harvestmen have eight long legs. They are known by the common name 'daddy-long-legs'.

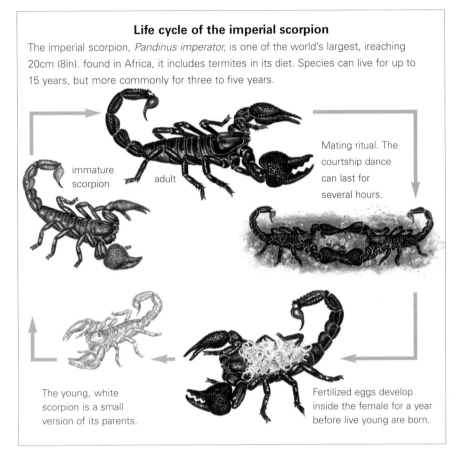

Life cycle of the imperial scorpion

The imperial scorpion, *Pandinus imperator*, is one of the world's largest, ireaching 20cm (8in). found in Africa, it includes termites in its diet. Species can live for up to 15 years, but more commonly for three to five years.

immature scorpion

adult

Mating ritual. The courtship dance can last for several hours.

The young, white scorpion is a small version of its parents.

Fertilized eggs develop inside the female for a year before live young are born.

the sac, the young attach themselves to the sides of the mother's abdomen. Usually there are fewer than two dozen young, but there can be more than one brood per year. The young moult three times, taking one to several years to reach adulthood. Some species disperse by clinging to the legs of passing flies

or other animals. Adults can live up to three years and typically overwinter in a silken cocoon.

Below: Pseudoscorpions are well named, for they resemble true scorpions in overall shape. However, they are much smaller and lack the long, stinging tail.

GLOSSARY

Abdomen Body region behind the thorax of an arthropod.

Antenna Sensitive narrow projections from the head. Also known as 'feelers'.

Aposematic Coloration on the body, warning that the animal is distasteful.

Appendage Extension of the body such as leg, wing or antenna.

Arachnid Member of the class Arachnida, which includes spiders, scorpions, mites and relatives.

Arthropod Invertebrates with jointed limbs.

Carnivore Animal that feeds on the flesh or tissues of another animal.

Carrion Dead animal flesh or tissues.

Caste Individuals specialized for a set task in a colony of social insects.

Cephalothorax Body region comprising a fused head and thorax, typically found in arachnids.

Cerci Paired, filamentous outgrowths from the tip of the abdomen.

Chelicerae Pincer-like mouthparts, typically found in arachnids.

Chemoreceptor Sense organ sensitive to traces of chemicals in the environment, as taste or smells.

Chitin The complex compound in the arthropod cuticle that gives it strength and rigidity.

Chrysalis The pupa of lepidopterans.

Cocoon Silk covering produced by some mature larvae before pupation. Also the silken egg sac of spiders.

Comb Rows of wax or papery brood cells in nests of social wasps and bees.

Communal Insects that share a nest. Each female rears her own brood.

Below: A newly hatched Heliconius charithonia *caterpillar on a passionflower tendril.*

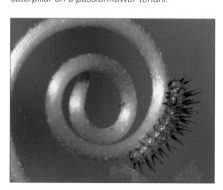

Compound eye Type of arthropod eye made up of many separate light-sensitive units.

Coxa The section of an arthropod leg that attaches to the body.

Crustacean Member of the class Crustacea.

Cryptic The patterning and colours of an animal that give it protection by allowing it to blend into a background.

Cuckoo-spit The foamy substance produced by some bugs to protect them from predators and from drying out.

Cuticle The outer layer of an arthropod's skin, forming the exoskeleton.

Diapause A resting period during development, triggered by specific conditions.

Diploid The normal state in which each cell nucleus contains two sets of chromosomes.

Diurnal Active mainly during the day.

Dorsal The back (usually the upper) surface of the body.

Drone Male honey bee.

Ecdysis Moulting of the old skin during arthropod growth.

Ectoparasite A parasite that lives and feeds on the surface of its host.

Elytra Modified hardened forewings that act as protective wing cases for the more delicate hindwings.

Endoparasite A parasite that lives and feeds inside the body of its host.

Endopterygote An insect in which wings develop inside its body. Involves a pupal stage and complete metamorphosis.

Exarate A pupa in which appendages are free of the rest of the body.

Exopterygote An insect in which the wings develop outside its body, during incomplete metamorphosis.

Exoskeleton The rigid outer body covering of an arthropod.

Femur The third joint of an insect leg, and usually the most powerful.

Gill Thin tissues that facilitate gaseous exchange during respiration.

Haemolymph The body fluid (blood) of an arthropod.

Hemimetabolous Insect with incomplete metamorphosis, with no pupal stage.

Above: A male polyphemus moth, Antheraea polyphemus, *displaying eye spots.*

Herbivore Feeding on plant material.

Hexapod A six-legged arthropod. Insects are the main hexapod class, the others being collembolans, diplurans and proturans.

Holometabolous Insect with complete metamorphosis, with a pupal stage.

Host The organism from which a parasite gains its nourishment.

Hymenopteran Member of the order Hymenoptera. Includes wasps, bees, ants, sawflies and wood wasps.

Imago The mature adult stage.

Instar Growth stage in the life of an immature arthropod, between moults.

Invertebrate Animals lacking a backbone.

Labium The lower lip in the mouthparts of an insect.

Larva The first juvenile stage in the life cycle of an animal that undergoes metamorphosis. The larva usually looks very different from the adult.

Lepidopteran Butterflies and moths, member of the order Lepidoptera.

Mandible Paired appendages near the mouth of an insect and some other arthropods, used for grasping and cutting food or for defence.

Maxilla Paired mouthparts behind the mandibles of an insect and some other arthropods, used for swallowing food. Sometimes the second pair of maxillae are fused to form the labium, or the maxillae may be modified into a proboscis.

Metamorphosis Development from egg to adult involving stages with different body shapes. May be

Above: A pill woodlouse, Armadillidium vulgare, *uncurling from a protective ball.*

complete where there is a pupal stage, or incomplete where the larva (or nymph) grows slowly to adult form.

Mimicry Where one species (the mimic) gains protection by resembling another species (the model). The mimic is often harmless, and the model may be distasteful or venomous.

Moulting The shedding its outer covering by a growing arthropod.

Myriapod Member of the superclass Myriapoda.

Nectar Sweet liquid produced by flowers to attract insect visitors. Nectar is a high-energy food exploited by many insects.

Nocturnal Active mainly at night.

Nymph The young larval stage of insects with incomplete metamorphosis.

Ocellus A simple eye with a single lens. Also used for the eye-like markings on the wings of some lepidopterans.

Ootheca Case containing the eggs of certain arthropods, especially orthopteran insects.

Ovipositor Egg-laying tube at the end of the abdomen of some female insects.

Paedogenesis Reproduction before the adult mature stage. Seen sometimes in insects where nymphs may be pregnant with the next generation.

Palp Appendage near the mouth of an arthropod, used for touching and tasting.

Parasite An organism that feeds on another (the host) without killing it.

Parasitoid An organism that feeds on another (the host) eventually causing its death. Many insect larvae are parasitoids because they feed on the body of the host, which later dies.

Parthenogenesis Reproduction without sex. The new individual grows from an unfertilized egg. Seen for example in certain generations of aphids, and also commonly in stick insects.

Pedipalp Appendage on the head of an arachnid, used either for grasping prey, or sometimes in reproduction.

Pheromone Chemical signal used, for example, by moths to find a mate, by ants to follow trails and by honey bees in communication.

Pollination Transfer of pollen to the female parts of a flower, often aided by visiting insects.

Predator An animal that feeds by catching other animals.

Proboscis The tube-like extended mouthparts of an insect, used for sucking in liquid food.

Proleg Outgrowths of the body of an insect larva that act as legs but which are not true limbs.

Pronotum Tough, shield-like cuticle covering the first segment of the insect thorax.

Prothorax The first of the three segments of the insect thorax.

Rostrum Beak-like mouthparts of bugs (Hemiptera).

Royal jelly Substance produced by worker honey bees and fed to larvae. Those larvae fed on royal jelly only develop into fertile queens.

Saprophage Animal that feeds on decaying matter.

Scale A flattened modified hair typically covering the wings of lepidoptera.

Segment A repeating body unit, most clearly seen in arthropods with long bodies, such as myriapods.

Social Organisms that live together in colonies.

Soldier A caste of worker in termites and ants that has a defensive role in the colony, usually with greatly enlarged jaws.

Spermatophore A packet of sperm produced by some arthropods.

Spinneret The organ in a spider's abdomen that produces silk. Also found in some insect larvae.

Spiracle The openings of the tracheae, along the sides of the arthropod body.

Stridulation Production of sound by rubbing together ridged surfaces, normally legs or wing cases. Typical of orthopterans.

Stylet Sharp, needle-like organ used for piercing. Found for example in the mouthparts of bugs, mosquitoes and fleas.

Subimago Adult-like stage in mayflies just before the full adult is formed. The subimago is duller than the adult, but like the adult it can fly.

Symbiosis Relationship between two organisms in which both partners benefit.

Synchronous Appearing at the same time, as in mass hatching of flying ants, for example.

Tarsus Final section of an insect leg, with claws at the tip.

Thorax The central body region of an arthropod, between the head and abdomen. The thorax bears the legs and wings (if present).

Tibia The fourth section of an insect leg, between the femur and the tarsus.

Trachea Small tubes lined with cuticle allowing gaseous exchange and opening through the spiracles.

Trochanter The short second section of an insect leg, between the coxa and femur.

Tubercle A small bump on the surface of the cuticle.

Venation The pattern of veins in the wing of an insect.

Venom Poison produced in special glands and used in defence or to immobilize or kill their prey. Typically found in many hymenopterans and spiders.

Viviparous Giving birth to live young.

Below: A European wasp, Vespula germanica, *at rest.*

INDEX

Below: Amazonian giant centipede

Below: A phasmid that resembles a leaf.

Below: A phasmid with camouflage patterns.

Below: Ladybird sitting on the bud of a thistle.

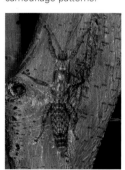

Below: Dragonfly next to its empty larval skin

Below: Butterfly emerging from its chrysalis.

Below: A grasshopper in mid-air.

Below: Banded damselfly with wings closed.

Below: A white spotted beetle on sandy soil.

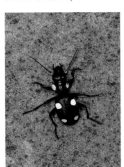

Below: Lacewing sucking nectar from flower.

PICTURE ACKNOWLEDGEMENTS

Alamy Page 52br, 54tc, 61tr, 69br, 73bl, bc and br, 75br.
Corbis Page 23tr, 36bl, 37bc, 37br, 53tr.
Fotolia Page 17cr and bc, 22bl, 23tc, 26br, 27tl, tr, bc, 28tr, bl and bc, 29bc, 30tr, 34tr, 44tr, 45br, 61bl, 67br, 70bl.
Istock Page 22bc, 41tc and tr, 50tr, 51br, 52bl, 54tr, 55tl, 59tr, 60bl, 68tr, 69tl.
NHPA Page 35bl, 46bl, 47tr, 49bl, 50bl.

Below: A stag beetle
showing claws on its feet.

Below: Camouflaged leaf
insect on a stick.

Below: A brown cat flea
clinging to hairs.

Below: A brown shield
bug sits on a leaf.

Below: An iridescent
green beetle on flowers.